Putting It Together

A Conversation Management Text

KEVIN MCCLURE

PRENTICE HALL REGENTS
UPPER SADDLE RIVER, NEW JERSEY 07458

Publisher: Arley Gray
Director of Production: Aliza Greenblatt
Editorial Production/Design Manager: Dominick Mosco
Manager of Development Services: Louisa B. Hellegers

Acquisitions Editor: Nancy Baxer
Development Editor: D. Andrew Gitzy
Production Editor; Interior Design, Composition: Noël Vreeland Carter
Production Coordinator: Ray Keating
Editorial Assistance: Sheryl Olinski
Art Director: Merle Krumper

Cover Design: Pakhaus Design
Illustrations: Peter Bono,
          Ruth Sofair Ketler

© 1996 by PRENTICE HALL REGENTS
Prentice-Hall, Inc.
A Simon & Schuster Company
Upper Saddle River, New Jersey 07458

Printed in the United States of America
10 9 8 7 6 5

0-13-128174-7

Prentice-Hall International (UK) Limited, *London*
Prentice-Hall of Australia Pty. Limited, *Sydney*
Prentice-Hall of Canada Inc. *Toronto*
Prentice-Hall Hispanoamericana, S.A., *Mexico*
Prentice-Hall of India Private Limited, *New Delhi*
Prentice-Hall of Japan, Inc. *Tokyo*
Simon & Schuster Asia Pte. Ltd., *Singapore*
Editora Prentice-Hall do Brasil, Ltda., *Rio de Janeiro*

CONTENTS

ACKNOWLEDGMENTS

I would like to thank the horde of people who have, over the past ten years, helped me bring this book into the world.

First and foremost are my mother and late father, Elizabeth and Gerald McClure, both of whom I resemble more and more as the years tumble by, and I don't even mind any more. My wife, June, and my son, Nathan, have helped greatly, the one by letting me escape my fair share of household duties on many Saturdays, and by helping me to understand that the way things *look* is important; the other by quickly learning that he shouldn't hit the power button on the computer while Daddy is working.

I would like to thank my professional colleagues, starting with my 11th and 12th grade English teacher, Mrs. Connie Gracy, who drove me to read and write more efficiently. I still write Gracy-style. I am deeply grateful to Dr. Charles Wrong, my history professor at the University of South Florida, for believing and helping me to believe that what we were doing was important. I would also like to thank my instructors in the Applied Linguistics Masters Program of the Department of Linguistics at the University of South Florida who rescued me from a life filled with odd jobs and odder people. One more year of taking inventory and I would have slashed my wrists. To these people, I would like to add the many overworked people at the Language Institute of Japan who patiently explained that there was such a thing as conversation management. Bill Harshbarger was particularly helpful in our one or two brief conversations about conversation. Francis Baily also gave me excellent advice on the finer points of curriculum development and humane management of human beings.

The advice of the staff at Temple University Japan was similarly invaluable. Susan Johnston and Michael Rost provided great support when I needed it. Nancy Baxer provided me with a means to bridge the gap between academia and the real world when she moved from TUJ to Prentice Hall. She also aided me by choosing Andrew Gitzy as my editor. So many of their ideas are in this book now, that where my work ends and theirs begins I haven't a clue.

Finally, I want to thank the entire staff at the ELS Language Center here in San Francisco, and Nancy Morrin in our executive offices for seeing my book project as something very positive rather than as something that would take me away from my normal duties. Their support was crucial.

Kevin McClure

INTRODUCTION

Putting It Together is designed to introduce intermediate students of English as a Foreign or Second Language to the basic idea of conversation management. Students who will benefit most from this text have a good foundation in grammar and reading. They have most likely studied all the basic and some of the more advanced forms of English grammar. They have done writing assignments that require multiple-clause sentences, and they have a good passive knowledge of English vocabulary. Their experience with speaking English, however, is very limited.

Great emphasis should be placed on using the skills learned in *Putting It Together* outside the framework of the text. In casual conversations and even in other classes, students should be given critical comments when they fail to use these skills. For example, if a student persists in nodding his or her head in agreement or to signal comprehension, even when it is obvious that nothing has been understood, the student should be challenged to explain what has been said. If the student is unable to do this, he or she should again be advised to ask for clarification— even if this means interrupting the speaker. Only through repeated reinforcement will students understand that they must use the management skills taught in this text to be successful in English conversation.

CHAPTER STRUCTURE

Each chapter of *Putting It Together* has four parts: 1) **Listening**; 2) **From the Dialogues**; 3) **Conversation Practice**; and 4) **Your Turn**. The teacher is advised to begin each chapter with a brief explanation of the theme, and of what the students should be able to do after they have completed the chapter. Often, exercises require students to use information from their personal experience. This approach helps the students form a strong bond with their classmates.

Listening

The **Listening** is designed to serve as a *brief* introduction to the conversation strategies, key phrases, grammar, and vocabulary of each chapter. Prior to beginning the listening exercises, students are asked discussion questions. These questions will help focus the student's attention on the chapter topic and solicit prior knowledge. A true/false comprehension exercise accompanies each dialogue. It is important to remember that this is *not* a listening text. The listening should be played a maximum of three times. The students will have the opportunity to examine the dialogues in greater detail in the first exercise of the **Conversation Practice**.

From the Dialogues

In this section, the students see a variety of words and phrases from the Listening Passage that can be used to talk about the chapter theme. They should not try to memorize these words; they should familiarize themselves with them on a recognition level. The instructor should go over each sentence or phrase to make sure that the students understand the vocabulary and idioms. Students should try to *use* as many of these words and phrases as possible in the **Conversation Practice** and **Your Turn** to gain total control over them.

Conversation Practice

Here, students are asked to act out the dialogues. They should be encouraged to ask questions about anything they do not understand. In some chapters, suggestions for expansion of the **From the Dialogues** vocabulary are made following this exercise. Students should use this vocabulary at their own discretion. The remainder of this section consists of controlled exercises. These exercises give students the chance to practice the vocabulary and idioms that were introduced in the preceding two sections.

Your Turn

The final section of each chapter allows the students to experiment with the language relatively free of constraint. Questionnaires and surveys of classmates' opinions and personal information help the students elicit *real* information about each other. Exercises are designed for students to practice idioms and vocabulary that will be truly useful outside the classroom. These exercises focus on communication. Grammar and vocabulary mistakes should be corrected only when they interfere with understanding. All information gathered in these exercises should be shared with the class to give the students one more chance to hear the key phrases and to use the key skills. Sharing personal information will also have the laudable effect of fostering a bond of understanding among the students.

The first four chapters of *Putting It Together* cover the mechanics of conversation management. They are longer than the later chapters because of their greater scope. The teacher should cover this material in detail as the basic skills needed throughout the text are presented there.

The chapters following the first four are of two types: skills-building chapters and chapters on specific topics. The skills-building chapters serve to reinforce and expand on those skills introduced at the beginning of the text. In the specific topic chapters, the emphasis is on cultural information and vocabulary and idioms commonly used when discussing the topic. The exercises contained there reinforce the students' ability to recognize and eventually use the new vocabulary. In the discussion sections of the specific topic chapters, the teacher should closely monitor the students' use of the vocabulary and offer detailed comments on inappropriate usage. The exercises in this text will undoubtedly stimulate more conversation and discussion if the students come from many different countries. However, if the students are homogeneous, the surveys and discussion questions can easily be adapted to ask for information from the different regions or cities within one country.

Suggestions for follow-up discussions, additional vocabulary, and cultural notes are offered for many of the chapters in the Appendix. The discussions may require an interest in controversial topics. If this interest is lacking in your students, feel free to make up your own topics or simply go on to the next chapter.

Postscript

I have had a very enjoyable time developing these materials and using them with students. Students who go through this book diligently (this means that they try to use the skills that they learn) will experience an increased ability to converse in English with native and non-native speakers. They should also be encouraged to have fun and learn about each other. The teacher should strive to provide an environment in which creativity and carefree social interaction can develop spontaneously. Students should be corrected mostly in the first three sections of the chapters. In the **Your Turn** sections, the students must be allowed to "let 'er rip!" Enjoy!

CHAPTER COMMENTS

Chapter 1: Asking for Clarification

This chapter requires students to take control of their English language learning experience. The basic skill offered can be summed up as follows: *If you do not understand something, you must ask a question; if you do understand, you must indicate that you understand.* Students are asked to turn their conversations in English into two-way processes—processes in which speakers cooperate with each other to communicate real information. While completing this chapter and after completing it, students should be given frequent feedback on their speaking behavior. They must be made to understand that, in real life situations, English-as-second-language students with poor grammar and limited vocabulary sometimes perform tasks more successfully than higher level students with considerably more vocabulary and grammar. The difference is behavior. If a student uses explanation strategies, repetition, and asks for clarification, chances for success are greatly enhanced. The exercises are straightforward; the teacher's main task is to convince the students that these skills are crucial to their success. After the students have finished this chapter, they should periodically be given some sort of information gap exercises for follow up.

Chapter 2: Getting Started

Greetings tend to be rather easy for most students. Openers and introductions, however, tend to be very tricky. Opening a topic is often a major hurdle for students. Idiomatic openers, such as *What's up?*, can also be very difficult.

Chapter 3: Keeping it Going

Most of the information in this chapter may be new for students, so it may be helpful to explain the purpose of the chapter and give a preview. If students use the strategies offered, they will be able to participate in a conversation without bearing the brunt of it. Using listener expressions encourages the speaker to talk more; the listener can sit back, relax, and utter an occasional *Oh really! How interesting! Tell me more!* Similarly, open questions act as a kind of "conversational judo" in which the responsibility for the conversation is thrust back at the speaker. These two skills used together allow a shy foreign student to participate minimally in a conversation with a native speaker. As the student gains confidence in his/her ability, he/she can begin to take the initiative. Just being able to survive a conversation with a native speaker can be a powerful confidence builder.

Chapter 4: Ending a Conversation

Students are generally familiar with a variety of closings, such as *Bye* and *Good night.* What students do not understand is that native speakers are not so direct in ending their conversations. A native speaker first signals an intention to withdraw and then maneuvers through series of pre-closings that may include greetings to loved ones, vague invitations for future activities, and/or the speaker's good wishes for the listener's future. All of this may take a considerable amount of time and may even involve re-starting the conversation. The conversation partner may resist ending the conversation by ignoring these indirect efforts. In this case, sterner measures are required. Ending a conversation can be far more complicated than students or even teachers generally realize.

Chapter 5: Weekends

Weekends are an all-pervasive passion for both students and teachers who would just as soon that it was Friday afternoon instead of Monday morning. After completing the chapter, teachers should spend a few minutes at the beginning of class on Mondays and Fridays discussing weekend activities. Attention should be given to key phrases: *Did you have a nice weekend?*, *What did you do?*, and *What are you going to do this weekend?* If students master these three expressions and the activities with the verb go, they will be much more able to participate in conversations on this topic.

Chapter 6: Weather

Weather is something that everyone is always talking about. In most cultures, it is a very typical daily topic that is totally innocuous. As such, it is the perfect topic for people who do not know each other. This chapter gives students one or two good openers. For example: *What's the weather going to be like tomorrow?* Students are also given enough vocabulary and knowledge of idioms that they can recognize what a native speaker is saying and give an appropriate response—even if the response is only a listener expression.

Chapter 7: Music

Music is important in all cultures. In this, more than in any other chapter, the discussion activities excite the students; they love talking about what kinds of music they like and who their favorite musicians or singers are. The focus is on asking for opinions, giving opinions, and stating preferences. Make sure that students use the vocabulary correctly in the discussion activities, monitor the students, and give them plenty of feedback at the end of the exercises.

Chapter 8: Explanations

The skills offered here should help students to explain what something is or to use these forms in circumlocution to reduce the number of conversational breakdowns. Teachers should focus on the student's ability to use these explanation forms in real conversations.

Chapter 9: Food

This chapter stimulates great amounts of speaking. Almost everyone loves to eat and talk about food. This is an excellent opportunity to practice giving and asking for opinions and stating preferences.

Chapter 10: Reduced Forms

Some students may feel that reduced forms are "bad English." The teacher may have to spend some time reassuring them that even well-educated people use reductions. It may be helpful to have students talk about reduced forms in their native languages. Samples of taped interviews from TV or radio may also help. One chapter cannot teach all such expressions. The chapter will, however, provide an introduction to reduced forms and give copious examples. Please note that the transcriptions of the reduced forms use rather arbitrary spelling. Moreover, variations occur depending on regional and national differences. Some people may say *Whaddya* for both *What are you* and *What do you*. Differences in dialects, such as between the U.S. and Australia, also complicate matters. The main idea, however, remains the same: all native speakers of English use some reduced forms. Students will need to know these forms to better understand native speakers.

Chapter 11: School

Students will probably have plenty to say in the **Your Turn** of this chapter. Some of it you may not want to hear, such as *What's your most boring subject?* The main focus is idioms and vocabulary. There are plenty of both, so do not be surprised if students do not master all of them. Emphasize vocabulary recognition and the use of those expressions and words that are most relevant to their student life. (If students are not in college or planning to go to college, vocabulary for graduate students may bore them.)

Chapter 12: Non-words

Students generally love learning the bizarre-sounding words from American English. They may practice these expressions for days afterward. Monitor students to make sure that they are not becoming confused between similar-sounding words, such as *Uh-huh*, *Uh-uh*, and *Uh-oh*.

Chapter 13: People

In this chapter, the focus is on words used to describe people; some of them are very negative. Although the teacher must keep the use of these words from descending into a vulgar name-calling contest, a certain amount of spirited teasing may be tolerable. Emphasis should also be placed on the positive words in this chapter.

Chapter 14: Conversational Expressions

This chapter covers several commonly misused expressions. Teachers should provide detailed explanations of the contexts in which the expressions are used appropriately. In future chapters, continue to listen carefully for proper usage.

Chapter 15: Feelings

This chapter asks students to divulge a certain amount of personal information about their feelings. Some care should be taken to insure that students do not become uncomfortable. Generally, the disclosure of feelings results in a more personal atmosphere in the class. Teachers should note that the dialogues are becoming much longer and more detailed. This trend will continue to build through the end of the book. Students may need more help understanding what is happening in the dialogues.

Chapter 16: Storytelling

Students are asked to relate an event using a chronological framework. Strong emphasis is placed on key expressions for time events and on expressions that may be used to introduce a story. Some of this vocabulary presented would rarely be used by native speakers, especially to the extent expected in this chapter. However, ESL/EFL students have grammar, pronunciation, and vocabulary problems that require the use of explicit markers (*first, takes place, about, then, finally*). As students improve, they will naturally develop the confidence to tell stories in a more natural style.

Chapter 17: Life

As with Chapter 15: *Feelings*, students are asked to disclose a certain amount of personal information. The vocabulary may be a bit daunting, but with some patience, students will learn to use *get married* and *married someone* correctly.

Chapter 18: Work

The materials presented here are primarily for students who are already engaged in some occupation. All students will, however, be employed one day, so the vocabulary is relevant to everyone. Similarly, all students can fantasize about the ideal job.

Chapter 19: Movies and TV

To be able to discuss movies and TV in English, students must learn to recognize the essential vocabulary and idioms. They must also be able to give details about why they like or dislike a particular movie or television program. This task may involve developing a critical faculty that they do not have in their native language. Students should devote significant energy to talking about scenery, directors and even cinematography.

Chapter 20: Telephone Language

Teachers should provide students with real practice. If you have a telephone in your office, have the students call to find out their grades on tests or papers. Have a student call you everyday to find out how you want the classroom set up (small groups, cassette recorder on the large desk in the front, chairs in a circle). If you are lucky enough to have a battery-operated phone set, you can make the roleplays much more realistic by having one phone in the room and one in the hall. The students can listen to the person in the room and guess what the other person is saying.

CHAPTER ONE

ASKING FOR CLARIFICATION

LISTENING

When you don't understand something in English, what do you do? Stay silent? Ask a question? Nod your head?

Listen to each dialogue and fill in the blanks with T (true) or F (false). Listen again to check your answers.

1. At a party

_____ The woman's name is Brigitte.

_____ The woman is French.

_____ The man's name is Paul.

_____ The man is from Smolensk.

_____ Smolensk is east of Moscow.

_____ Smolensk is on the river Niger.

_____ Brigitte is from Atlanta.

_____ Atlanta is in the western United States.

_____ Georgia is north of Florida.

2. Making a plane reservation.

_____ The man would like to fly to Dallas.

_____ He would like to fly on the fifth of October.

_____ He would like to fly in the afternoon.

_____ There is a flight at 10:14.

_____ The man's name is John Borlowski.

_____ The man lives at 1416 15th St.

_____ His telephone number is 431-9867.

FROM THE DIALOGUES

Study the vocabulary.

ASKING FOR CLARIFICATION

Pardon me? / Excuse me?
I'm sorry, but I didn't catch that.
Could you repeat that?
Could you spell your last name**?**
How do you spell that?
What does Dneiper **mean?**

REPEATING INFORMATION AS A QUESTION

1460 50th St.**?**
8976**?**

PARAPHRASING INFORMATION TO CHECK IT

So . . . that's John Borlowski, flying to Oklahoma City from Dallas on Friday, October 5, at 10:40.

TELLING SOMEONE THAT THEY'VE UNDERSTOOD

Yes, that's right.
Yes, that's correct.
Correct.

CORRECTING MISTAKES

No, I'm sorry, but I think that you've made a mistake.
No, actually it's in the middle of Georgia.
Uh, no. That's not quite right.

WH-QUESTIONS FOR CLARIFICATION

✔ *Use rising intonation.*

What is it in the middle of**?**
When is the flight**?**

CONFIRMING NUMBERS

Did you say four-zero **or** one-four**?**
That's one-five**?**

CONVERSATION PRACTICE

1. Turn to page 11 and read each dialogue in pairs. Ask your teacher to explain any vocabulary or grammar you do not understand.

2. In pairs, write a sentence asking for clarification. Then read the conversations to the class.

Examples: A: My telephone number is 228-6731.
B: *Could you repeat that?*

A: I'm staying at the Abyssinia Hotel.
B: *How do you spell that?*

228 – 6731

1. A: My name is Denise Ruggiero.

   B: _____

2. A: Paris is in the north part of France on the Seine.

   B: _____

3. A: I'm from Sri Lanka.

   B. _____

4. A: Her phone number is 935-4926.

   B: _____

5. A: The movie is called "Gone with the Window."

   B: _____

6. A: He lives in Indianapolis.

   B: _____

*3. In pairs, write a question for each sentence by repeating information. Then read the conversations to the class. **NOTE:** Use rising intonation in questions.*

Examples: A: My name is Albert.   A: I'm arriving at 9:00.   A: My father lives in Spain.
B: *Albert?*   B: *9:00?*   B: *In Spain?*
A: Yes, that's right.   A: Yes, that's correct.   A: Uh-huh.

1. A: My mother is flying to Hawaii on Thursday.

   B: _____

   A: Yes, that's right.

2. A: My phone number is 228-6009.

   B: _____

   A: Yes, that's correct.

3. A: I first came to the U.S. in 1985.

   B: _____

   A: Yes.

4. A: I'm staying at the Regency Hotel.

   B: _____

   A: Uh-huh.

5. A: I'm from New Hampshire.

   B: _____

   A: Yes, that's right.

4. In pairs, write corrections for the following mistakes. Then read the conversations to the class.

Examples: A: I'm leaving on Tuesday at 4:50.
                 B: OK, Tuesday at 4:15.
                 A: *No, I'm sorry, but I think that you've made a mistake. I'm leaving at 4:50.*

                 A: I'm from Paris.
                 B: So you speak French?
                 A: *No, that's not quite right. I'm actually from Paris, Texas.*

Austria or
Australia?

1. A: I'm from Austria.

   B: Did you say Australia?

   A: _____

2. A: I'm going to be living in Chicago for four weeks.

   B: That's four months in Chicago?

   A: _____

3. A: My name is Jose.

   B: It's nice to meet you Juan.

   A: _____

4. A: My mother will arrive on Friday the 30th.

   B: She's coming Friday the 13th?

   A: _____

5. *In pairs, write WH-questions for each conversation. Then read the conversations to the class.*

Examples: A: I was born in Minnesota.
B: *Where were you born?*
A: In Minnesota.

A: I would like a ticket on flight #34.
B: *What flight was that?*
A: #34. It's going to London.

A: I'm leaving on Tuesday.
B: *When are you leaving?*
A: On Tuesday.

A: John is coming on Friday.
B: *Who is coming on Friday?*
A: John is.

I saw a penguin in his bathroom!

1. A: I saw a penguin in his bathroom!
   B: What _____
   A: A penguin.

2. A: I'm going home on Thursday.
   B: When _____
   A: On Thursday.

3. A: I'm going to Venezuela next week.
   B: Where _____
   A: To Venezuela.

4. A: I'm going to buy a new stereo.
   B: What _____
   A: A new stereo.

5. A: Marie is from Senegal.
   B: _____
   A: Marie is.

6. A: The weather is beautiful in Australia.

B: _____

A: In Australia.

7. A: He's flying to Vancouver next week.

B: _____

A: Next week.

6. *In pairs, write questions to confirm numbers for each conversation. Then read the conversations to the class.*

Examples: A: John is 18 years old.
B: *Did you say one-eight or eight-zero?*
A: One-eight.

A: It was 17 days ago.
B: *That was one-seven?*
A: Yes, that's right.

PRONUNCIATION NOTE	
Teens	Tens
(2 long syllables)	(1 long and one short syllable)
THIR TEEN	**THIR** ty
FOUR TEEN	**FOUR** ty

Practice saying the following:	
15	50
16	60
17	70

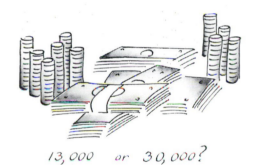

13,000   or   30,000?

1. A: I have $13,000.

B: _____

A: I said $13,000.

2. A: There are 50 people waiting to see you.

B: _____

A: No, five-zero.

3. A: I live on 40th St.

B: _____

A: Yes, that's correct.

4. A: She's 18 years old.

B: _____

A: One-eight.

7. Put the conversation in the correct order by numbering the sentences. The first one is done for you. When you finish, compare your answers with a classmate's answers.

_____ Certainly, K-O-M-A-T-E-R.

_____ What time was that?

_____ Eight-fifteen.

_____ Excuse me?

_____ Komater.

_____ There will be four people.

_____ And what is your name?

_____ All right, Mr. Komater . . . that's an eight-fifteen reservation for four.

___1___ Coleto's Restaurant. May I help you?

_____ Could you spell that please?

_____ Yes, that's right. Thank you

_____ Yes, I'd like to make an eight-fifteen reservation for dinner.

_____ How many are in your party?

_____ How many people will come?

YOUR TURN

1. Plan a Trip

Work in pairs.

Student A is a travel agent. You must ask Student B for information about the trip he/she wants to plan. Use the questions below and <u>confirm all the information</u>.

Student B wants to plan a trip. You must answer Student A's questions. Do not look at the questions. When you have finished, switch roles.

1. What is your name?
2. How many people will be traveling with you? What are their names?
3. Where would you like to go?
4. When would you like to leave? When would you like to return?
5. How much money do you have to spend on the trip?
6. Would you like smoking or non-smoking seats on planes, buses, trains, etc.?
7. Do you want first-class, business class, or tourist (coach) seats?
8. Could you give me your address/telephone number?

2. Take a Class

Work in pairs.

Student A works in a university office and registers students for classes. You must ask Student B for information about the class he/she wants to take. Use the questions below and <u>confirm all the information</u>.

Student B would like to sign up for an evening class. You must answer Student A's questions. Do not look at the questions. When you have finished, switch roles.

1. What is your name?
2. What class would you like to sign up for? (English 101, Computers 202, etc.)
3. Would you like the 6:00 p.m. or the 7:30 p.m. class?
4. Would you prefer a Monday-Wednesday class or a Tuesday-Thursday class?
5. Have you graduated from high school? Have you ever studied in a college or university? If so, where and for how long?
6. Would you prefer to study at our downtown campus or at the main campus outside of the city?
7. Are you interested in taking this class for college credit (for a degree, such as a B.A.) or on a non-credit basis?
8. What is your address/telephone number?
9. Do you have a telephone number at work?

3. Survey

Ask five members of your class for the information in the chart below. Be sure to ask for clarification when you need it. When you finish, discuss your answers with your classmates. What areas or countries are your classmates from? How close to your school do they live?

What is your name?	What country are you from?	What is your present address?	What is your telephone number?
1.			
2.			
3.			
4.			
5.			

ASKING FOR CLARIFICATION TRANSCRIPT

1. At a party.

Brigitte: Hi! I'm Brigitte.

Peter: Excuse me?

Brigitte: Brigitte, it's a French name.

Peter: Are you French?

Brigitte: No, actually I'm an American. Only my name is French.

Peter: I'm Peter.

Brigitte: It's nice to meet you Peter. Where are you from?

Peter: I'm from Russia.

Brigitte: Really? What city are you from?

Peter: Smolensk.

Brigitte: I'm sorry, but I didn't catch that.

Peter: Smolensk. It's west of Moscow on the Dneiper.

Brigitte: What does Dneiper mean?

Peter: It's a river.

Brigitte: Oh, I see. How do you spell that?

Peter: It's spelled D-N-E-I-P-E-R.

Brigitte: I think I've heard of it. (*pause*)

Peter: What city are you from?

Brigitte: I'm from Atlanta.

Peter: That's on the Atlantic Ocean?

Brigitte: No, actually it's in the middle of Georgia!

Peter: What is it in the middle of?

Brigitte: Georgia.

Peter: I'm sorry, but I don't really know the U.S. very well. Is it in the north or south?

Brigitte: It's in the south, just north of Florida.

Peter: Oh, now I understand. It's north of Cuba!

Brigitte: Yes. That's right. (*pause*)

Peter: Well, it's been very nice talking to you. It's getting rather late and I should be leaving.

Brigitte: Maybe we'll meet again.

Peter: I hope so. Good night.

Brigitte: Good night.

2. Making a plane reservation.

Clerk: Oklahoma Airlines. May I help you?

John: Yes, I'd like to fly from Dallas to Mexico City.

Clerk: And when would you like to go?

John: The fifth of October.

Clerk: That's Friday the fifteenth?

John: No, I'm sorry, but I think you've made a mistake. That's Tuesday the fifth.

Clerk: O.K. Tuesday the fifth. What time of day would you like to fly?

John: I'm sorry, but the phone connection isn't very good. Could you repeat that?

Clerk: What time of day would you like to fly? Morning, afternoon or evening?

John: Oh, I'd like to fly in the morning.

Clerk: We have a flight at ten forty.

John: When is the flight?

Clerk: Ten-forty.

John: Did you say four-zero or one-four?

Clerk: Four-zero.

John: OK, I'd like one seat on that flight.

Clerk: Could you give me your name?

John: Borlowski. John Borlowski.

Clerk: Could you spell your last name?

John: B-O-R-L-O-W-S-K-I

Clerk: And your address?

John: 1460 15th St. in Dallas.

Clerk: 1460 50th St.?

John: Uh, no. That's not quite right. It's not 50th St. It's 15th St.

Clerk: That's one-five?

John: Yes, that's correct.

Clerk: And your telephone number?

John: 431-8976

Clerk: Pardon me?

John: 431-8976

Clerk: 8976?

John: Yes, that's right.

Clerk: So . . . that's John Borlowski, flying to Mexico City from Dallas on Tuesday, October 5th at 10:40.

John: Yes, that's right.

Clerk: Your telephone number is 431-8976 and your address in Dallas is 1460 15th Street.

John: Correct.

Clerk: All right Mr. Borlowski, you should be at the check-in counter one hour before the flight.

John: Thank you very much.

Clerk: Thank you.

CHAPTER TWO

GETTING STARTED

LISTENING

Look at the picture. What do you say to greet people you know? What kinds of things do you say to someone you are just meeting?

Listen to each dialogue and fill in the blanks with T (true) or F (false). Listen again to check your answers.

1. Steve goes into his boss' office.

_____ Marilyn has just finished her degree.

_____ Steve has a plan to increase production.

2. At work

_____ Ms. Johnson had to work on the weekend.

_____ Sally and her boss have a very informal relationship.

3. Two high school students meet.

_____ Carl got a haircut.

_____ Carl went to the movies the night before.

4. Tomonori and Jae meet at a museum.

_____ Tomonori was late.

_____ Tomonori and Jae just met today.

5. Three people meet at a restaurant.

_____ Bob and Carol are going to be married.

_____ Bob and Marty are old friends.

6. At a supermarket

_____ Fred and Joe planned to meet.

_____ Joe's wife just got a promotion.

_____ Fred has children.

7. Two couples meet at a dance.

_____ Mary is married to Ralph.

_____ Sarah and Mary are old friends.

_____ Sarah is a jewelry designer.

_____ Larry is an editor for Regis Publications.

FROM THE DIALOGUES

Study the vocabulary.

GREETINGS

Formal
> **Good morning,** Ms. Johnson.
> **Good morning,** Sally.

Informal
> Joe! **I didn't expect to see you here.**
> **Hey,** Fred.
> **Hi** Carl.
> **Sorry I'm late.**
> Bob, **I'm glad that you could come!**
> Mary, **it's nice to see you here.**
> Sarah! **What a nice surprise!**

> **Note:** It's nice to *see* you. (you already know the person)
> It's nice to *meet* you. (you don't know the person)

INTRODUCTIONS

> **Let me introduce you.** Bob, **this is** Carol.
> **Nice to meet you.**
> **Nice to meet you too,** Bob.

> **I'd like to introduce you to my new assistant. This is** Marilyn Boggs.
> **It's a pleasure to meet you,** Ms. Boggs.

> **Hey, I'd really like you to meet** my husband. Larry, **this is** my old friend Sarah.
> **I'm happy to meet you,** Sarah.
> **Hi,** I'm Ralph.

CONVERSATION OPENERS

General Questions
> **How're you doing?**
> **How are you today?**
> **Well, how have you been?**
> **How are you doing?**
> **What's up? = What's happening? = What's going on?**

> **Note:** Be careful! *How* are you doing?
> and
> *What* are you doing? sound similar.

Specific Questions (you already have some information)
> **How's** Isabella**?**
> **Say, how're** the kids**?**

> **Did you** get a haircut**?**
> **Did you** have a nice weekend**?**

Statements (you have a topic)
> Hey, there was a great movie on TV last night.
> Marty has told me a great deal about you.
> Ms. Smith has told me about your plans to increase production.
> Sara is a jewelry designer.
> Ralph works for Regis Publications. He's an editor.

CONVERSATION PRACTICE

1. *Turn to page 23 and read each dialogue in pairs. Divide into groups of three for dialogues five and six. Dialogue seven is for four people. Ask your teacher to explain any vocabulary or grammar you do not understand.*

VOCABULARY EXPANSION

Study the additional vocabulary.

CONVERSATION OPENERS

General Questions

Have you seen any good movies recently?

What have you been doing lately?

Do you ever go to the park?

Specific Questions

Is your mother feeling better?

Did you go to the movie with Mark?

Are you still planning to go to China?

Statements

I went to a great party last night.

I met a really interesting woman!

Mary went to Europe.

SPECIAL EXPRESSIONS FOR OPENING TOPICS

I have something to tell you.
I've been meaning to tell you about the new computer I bought.
You'll never guess what I found for sale in the newspaper.
Guess who's in my biology class.
I heard that you were moving to Thailand.
Did you hear that our team won the game last night?
I've got some news.
Something really strange happened today!
What do you think about the election?

2. In pairs, read each situation and circle the best answer.

1. It is 9:00 Wednesday morning in your office. You are at your desk. Your boss comes in. You see her every day, Monday through Friday. You have a formal/businesslike relationship with her. What do you say?

    a. Hey, how're you doing?

    b. Good morning, Ms. Schmid.

    c. Hi, what's up?

    d. Hello. How have you been?

    e. What have you been doing?

2. You are walking down a street and you see your old friend Jack. You have not seen him for about ten years. You were best friends in high school. What do you say?

    a. How have you been?

    b. Good morning. How have you been doing?

    c. It's nice to see you again.

    d. Jack, I can't believe it. It's wonderful to see you again!

    e. What have you been doing!

3. Match the sentences in Column One with the sentences in Column Two. The first one is done for you.

Column One

___g___ Good morning.

_____ Jose, I'd like you to meet Alicia.

_____ How are you?

_____ Abdul, this is Joe. He's from Florida.

_____ Did you have a nice weekend?

_____ What's up?

_____ It's nice to meet you.

Column Two

a. Yes, I did. Thanks.

b. Nothing much.

c. Really? It must seem very cold to you here.

d. Nice to meet you.

e. It's nice to meet you, too.

f. Fine, thanks.

g. Good morning.

4. *In pairs, read the following situations. Then write three different openers for each. Read your answers to the class.*

I just got back from Mexico!

Example: You are with three close friends. You have just returned from a three-week vacation in Mexico. You had a wonderful time.

1. *I just got back from Mexico.*
2. *Well, how have you been?*
3. *I had a wonderful vacation!*

1. You are talking with Makoto. Last week, he told you that Kumiko, his wife, was sick.

_____

_____

_____

2. You are talking with Maria. She is wearing a beautiful gold necklace.

_____

_____

_____

3. You are with two friends. You want to talk about baseball. Your favorite baseball team, the Dodgers, beat the Yankees last night.

_____

_____

_____

4. You are at a party with a group of people you do not know very well. The talking stops for a moment. You want to talk about the new symphony orchestra in your city.

_____

_____

_____

5. You are with some old friends. Another friend told you that they have just come back from a vacation in Japan.

_____

_____

_____

5. *Put the conversations in the correct order by numbering the sentences. When you finish, compare your answers with a classmate's answers.*

1. _____ Well, Kim and I went to a great movie last night.

   __1__ Hi, Harry. How're you doing?

   _____ Oh, yeah? What was it?

   _____ Not bad. What's new?

   _____ Nothing much. What's new with you?

   _____ *Attack of the Frog Men.* It was exciting. You should see it sometime.

2. _____ Not bad. Hey, I heard that you were going to Mexico.

   _____ Thanks!

   _____ Hi, Lilliana. How have you been?

   _____ Well, have fun!

   _____ Yeah, we're leaving next week.

   _____ Fine, thanks and you?

3. _____ Mary's going to be in your department working as a computer programmer.

   _____ Fine, Ching. How are you?

   _____ It's nice to meet you, Mary.

   _____ Great! Tomas, I'd like you to meet our newest employee, Mary Bradshaw.

   _____ It's nice to meet you too, Tomas.

   _____ Good morning, Tomas. How are you today?

4. _____ Pretty good, actually. How are you?

   _____ Hey Miguel, how've you been?

   _____ Nice to meet you, Miguel.

   _____ Almost five years.

   _____ Not bad. Hey, I'd like you to meet my husband, Ralph. Ralph, this is Miguel. He's an old friend from school.

   _____ Nice to meet you too. So, how long have you been married?

YOUR TURN

1. Interview and Introductions

In pairs, briefly interview a partner. Try to find out as much information as possible about your partner's life.

Sample Questions for the Interview

What is your name?	How long have you been in this city?
Where are you from?	How long have you been in this school?
Where do you live?	Why did you come to study here?
What are your hobbies?	Do you have a job?
What sports do you like?	What is your city/country like?
What kind of music do you like?	

Go around the room and meet other pairs. Each student should take a turn introducing his/her partner. Give as much of the information from the interview as possible.

Example:

You: I'd like to introduce you to Joao. He's from Brazil. He came here to study Business English. He likes to play baseball.

Other student: Nice to meet you.

Joao: Nice to meet you, too.

BRAZIL

Joao is from Brazil

2. Breaking the Ice

Make a list of some topics that interest you. For example:

your favorite musical group
a movie you saw
a book you read
your favorite sports team
your hobby
a current event (national or international news)

Write an opener for each topic.

Examples: I saw a great movie last night.
The orchestra's playing Mozart tonight.
Do you like sports?
What is your favorite book?

In pairs or small groups, stand up and have conversations. Remember to use a greeting and an opener.

I saw a great movie last night.

3. Survey

Ask five members of your class the question in the chart below. Try to list at least five subjects. When you finish, compare your list with your classmates' lists. Discuss which topics were most popular with your class.

Student Name	What topics do you like to talk about?
1.	
2.	
3.	
4.	
5.	

GETTING STARTED TRANSCRIPT

1. Steve goes into his Boss' office.

Boss: Steve, come on in. I'd like to introduce you to my new assistant. (*pause*) This is Marilyn Boggs. She just finished her M.B.A. at Harvard.

Steve: It's a pleasure to meet you, Ms. Boggs.

Marilyn: Oh, please call me Marilyn.

Steve: And please call me Steve!

Marilyn: O.K., Steve. I'm looking forward to working with you. Ms. Smith has told me about your plans to increase production.

2. At work.

Sally: Good morning, Ms. Johnson.

Ms. Johnson: Good morning, Sally. How are you today?

Sally: Fine thank you. And you?

Ms. Johnson: O.K., I guess.

Sally: Did you have a nice weekend?

Ms. Johnson: No, not really. I had some paperwork to catch up on. How was yours?

Sally: I went skiing in Aspen.

Ms. Johnson: That sounds very nice. (*pause*) Could you get me the MacDonald file?

Sally: Here it is.

3. Two high school students meet.

Warren: Hi Carl.

Carl: Hi Warren. What's up?

Warren: Nothin' much. Umm, did you get a haircut?

Carl: Yeah, I did.

Warren: It looks great!

Carl: Thanks. Hey, there was a great movie on TV last night!

Warren: What was it?

Carl: *The Slasher.* . . .

4. Tomonori and Jae meet at a museum.

Tomonori: Sorry I'm late, Jae!

Jae: It's O.K., Tomonori. I just got here myself. Well, how have you been?

Tomonori: Pretty well, but I've been so busy lately that I haven't had a chance to relax.

Jae: Then, I hope you'll enjoy this exhibit on South American art.

5. Three people meet at a restaurant.

Marty: Bob, I'm glad that you could come!

Bob: Well, I really wanted to meet your fiancee.

Marty: Let me introduce you. Bob, this is Carol. We've been going out for over a year now.

Bob: Nice to meet you.

Carol: Nice to meet you too, Bob. Marty has told me a great deal about you.

Marty: That's true Bob, I told her all about high school and college.

Bob: And she still wanted to meet me?

Carol: Of course!

6. At a supermarket.

Fred: Joe! I didn't expect to see you here.

Joe: Hey, Fred. How're you doing?

Fred: Not bad. Not bad at all. How about you?

Joe: Oh, I'm slowing down a bit, but I'm getting along.

Fred: Glad to hear it! How's your wife?

Joe: Isabella's just fine. She got another promotion at work.

Fred: Really!

Joe: Yeah, she's a district manager now.

Fred: Well, that's great!

Joe: Say, how're the kids?

Fred: Well, Steve's in college now.

Joe: I can't believe it! Time really flies . . .

7. Two couples meet at a dance.

Sarah: Mary, it's nice to see you here.

Mary: Sarah! What a nice surprise! Hey, I'd really like you to meet my husband.

Sarah: I'd love to meet him. You've told me so much about him!

Mary: Hey, Larry. Could you come over here for a second? (*pause*) Larry, this is my old friend Sarah. We haven't seen each other in ages!

Larry: I'm happy to meet you, Sarah.

Mary: Sarah is a jewelry designer. She has her jewelry in all the best shops.

Larry: Really! I'd love to see some of your jewelry some time.

Sarah: Here comes my husband. (*pause*) Honey, this is my old friend Mary and her husband Larry.

Ralph: Hi, I'm Ralph.

Larry: Nice to meet you, Ralph.

Mary: Nice to meet you.

Sarah: Ralph works for Regis Publications. He's an editor.

Larry: Really, what kind of things do you edit?

Ralph: Mostly travel magazines. . . .

CHAPTER THREE

KEEPING IT GOING

LISTENING

Look at the pictures. In each, someone is describing past activities. Where was each person? What was he/she doing? Do you think each person was enjoying him/herself or not?

Listen to each dialogue and fill in the blanks with T (true) or F (false). Listen again to check your answers.

1. *Two students meet after summer vacation.*

_____ Mary was very busy during the summer.

_____ Mary helped her mother with the furniture in her office.

_____ Mary feels that she understands her mother better now.

_____ Paul worked in a lumber mill for two months.

_____ Paul spent three weeks in Europe.

_____ Paul did not really like Switzerland.

_____ Paul liked Italian food.

_____ The people in Italy were not very friendly.

2. *A boy is describing his day to his father.*

_____ Billy went hiking with Tommy and Joey.

_____ The boys saw some rabbits.

_____ They went swimming in Miller Lake.

_____ The weather was hot.

_____ Miller Lake has an island in it.

_____ When it began to rain, the boys ran home.

_____ Billy's father had a very interesting day.

FROM THE DIALOGUES

Study the vocabulary.

LISTENER EXPRESSIONS

Listener expressions encourage the speaker to continue.

Positive

I'm glad to hear that!
That's great!
That's wonderful!
That must have been wonderful . . .

Neutral   Sympathy   Other
Uh-huh.   **I'm sorry to hear that.**   **Really?**
               That's too bad!   **So, it sounds like you had** an
                                                        adventurous day!
                                                   Sounds boring!

AVOIDING SILENCE

When someone asks you a question and you understand it, but you need time to think, **say something!**

Well, . . .
Well, let me see . . .
Hmmmm, well, . .
Well, let me think . . .

OPEN QUESTIONS

Open questions have many possible answers. They are good for encouraging listeners. When answering questions, you should give as complete an answer as possible.

Opinion Questions   Possible Answers
How was your summer?   It was busy / great / terrible / etc.
How was that?   It was nice / pretty good / etc.
So, how was Switzerland?   It was fantastic / beautiful / etc.
How did you **like** Italy?   The food was incredible./
                                           The people were very friendly./ etc.
How was your day Billy?   Pretty good. / etc.

Description Questions   Possible Answers
What was your summer like?   I worked down at the mill./
                                           I spent two weeks in Europe.
What was it like?   It was fantastic./ I loved the architecture of
                                               the cities. . . .
What's Miller Lake **like** nowadays?   It's really deep and has an island in the
                                               middle of it.

> **Note:** Be careful with: *How* did you *like* _____ ? (opinion)
> and *What* was _____ *like*? (description)

CONVERSATION PRACTICE

1. Turn to page 34 and read each dialogue in pairs. Ask your teacher to explain any vocabulary or grammar you do not understand.

> **VOCABULARY EXPANSION**
>
> *Study the additional vocabulary.*
>
> **AVOIDING SILENCES**
> **That's a difficult question . . .**
> **Uh . . .**
>
> **OPEN QUESTIONS**
> Opinion Questions
>   **What was your opinion of** Korea?
>   **What did** you **think of** Norway?
>   **Why did** you go to China?
> Description Questions
>   **Could you tell me about** your country?
>   **How would you describe** Senegal?

2. In pairs, write a listener expression for each sentence. Then read the conversations to the class.

Examples: A: My dog died yesterday.
                 B: *I'm really sorry to hear that.*

                  A: I got a raise at work!
                  B: *That's great!*

1. A: My wife and I just had a baby!

   B: _____

2. A: I have to write an essay for my English class.

   B: _____

3. A: My boss gives me too much work!

   B: _____

4. A: I went to Greece for two weeks.

   B:_____

5. A: I'm going to the movies tonight with my boyfriend.

   B:_____

6. A: I lost my job!

   B:_____

7. A: I had a great weekend.

   B:_____

8. A: I was accepted by Harvard University!

   B:_____

3. Put an X in front of any open question.

_____ What is your name?   _____ What is your family like?

_____ What is your country like?   _____ What is your favorite kind of music?

_____ How old are you?   _____ How was your vacation?

_____ How do you like the United States? _____ Do you like jazz?

_____ Why did you come to this school to study? _____ What do you like about Brazil?

4. In pairs, read the following situations. Write one opinion and one description question for each. Then write a possible answer for each question. Read your answers to the class.

Examples: You meet a friend who has just returned from New York.
                 A: _How did you like New York?_ (opinion)
                 B: _I really liked it!_
                 A: _What was New York like?_ (description)
                 B: _It was really big and crowded._

   1. Your brother went to a concert last night.

      A: _____

      B: _____

      A: _____

      B: _____

   2. You meet a friend who has just returned from India.

      A: _____

      B: _____

      A: _____

      B: _____

3. Your mother and father went to a new restaurant last week.

A: _____

B: _____

A: _____

B: _____

5. *In pairs, take turns asking and answering the questions. When answering, use the expressions to avoid silence.*

Example: A: How did you like the movie?

B: *Hmmm . . . well . . . , it was too violent.*

1.   What was the beach like?

2.   How did you like Thailand?

3.   What did you like best in Egypt?

4.   What was Mexico like?

What was the beach like?

6. *When responding to questions, give a complete answer. Look at example and note Student B's three different answers.*

Example: Poor

A: What was Japan like?

B: *Great!*

A: *Uh-huh.*

Better

A: What was Japan like?

B: *It was great. The people were very friendly.*

A *So, it sounds like you had a good time.*

Best:

A: What was Japan like?

B: *It was great. The people were very friendly. I went there on vacation. The temples and shrines in Kyoto are really beautiful.*

A: *(many possible responses)*

In pairs, read the sentences and write complete answers. Then read your answers to the class.

1. A: How was your last vacation?

B: _____

_____

_____

_____

2. A: How do you like your classes?

    B: _____

    _____

    _____

    _____

3. A: What do you think of pop music?

    B: _____

    _____

    _____

    _____

4. A: Could you tell me about your country?

    B: _____

    _____

    _____

    _____

7. *Put the conversation in the correct order by numbering the sentences. When you finish, compare your answers with a classmates' answers.*

_____ Hmmm . . . well, the pool was small, but it was clean . . . and it was only a five minute walk to the ocean.

_____ Bye.

_____ So how was the weather?

_____ I'll do that. See you later.

_____ Not bad. How're you doing?

_____ Uh-huh, it was really cheap.

_____ It sounds great. Hey, I've got to get to class. Why don't you give me a call the next time you go?

_____ Well, it was clear, really hot, and humid, but the water was nice and cold, and the surf was incredible!

_____ I'm doing great. I just got back from the beach.

_____ That's good. I hate it when the water is too warm. How long were you there?

__1__ Hey, John. How're you doing today?

_____ We stayed for three days, two nights.

_____ A cheap one, huh? What was it like?

_____ The beach? Did you stay in a hotel?

YOUR TURN

1. Tell a Story

*In groups of three or four, tell a story. As each speaker is telling his/her story, the listeners must respond with listener expressions (**Uh-huh, Really?, That's too bad.**).*

> **Possible topics**
>
> My most interesting experience.
> My most terrible experience.
> My trip to _____.

My most terrible experience

2. My Imaginary Vacation

*Work in pairs or small groups. Imagine that you recently took a vacation. Take turns telling your partner(s) about your trip. The speaker should answer the questions below. The listeners must ask Open Questions (**What was the _____ like?**) and use Listener Expressions (**Really? How terrible**).*

> Where did you go? (country, city, area)
> What did you do? (skiing, swimming, scuba diving, hiking, riding motorcycles)
> Who did you meet?
> What was the country/city like? (mountainous, beach, dry, humid, flat, crowded, empty, rainy, green, desert)
> What was the food like? (spicy, bland, rich, mostly seafood, lots of rice and vegetables
> What were the people like? (friendly, indifferent, boring, poor, aggressive, handsome/ beautiful)
> What was your favorite part of the vacation?
> What was your least favorite part of the vacation?

3. Survey

Ask five members of your class for the information in the chart below. When you finish, discuss your answers with your classmates.

Name?	Where do you live?	Why did you come to this city?	How do you like living in this city?	What is your hometown?
1.				
2.				
3.				
4.				
5.				

KEEPING IT GOING TRANSCRIPT

1. Two students meet after summer vacation.

Paul: Mary! I've been looking for you!

Mary: Paul! It's so nice to see you again!

Paul: How was your summer?

Mary: Well, let me see. It was certainly busy!

Paul: What did you do?

Mary: Well, I worked full time at my mother's office helping her with the books.

Paul: How was that?

Mary: It was nice to get to know my mother better.

Paul: Uh-huh.

Mary: I had always seen her only as my mother. Now, I understand her better.

Paul: That's great! I was pretty busy myself.

Mary: What was your summer like?

Paul: Well, I worked down at the mill cutting lumber for the first two months. . . .

Mary: Uh-huh.

Paul: . . . and then I spent two weeks in Europe.

Mary: Where did you go?

Paul: Italy, France, and Switzerland.

Mary: Really? What was it like?

Paul: Hmmm, well, it was fantastic! I loved the architecture of the cities and the museums the best.

Mary: So how was Switzerland?

Paul: It was really beautiful. Lots of mountains and lakes!

Mary: Uh-huh. How did you like Italy?

Paul: Well . . . the food was incredible.

Mary: That's wonderful!

Paul: And the people were very friendly.

Mary: I'm glad to hear that! Maybe I'll go to Italy next year.

Paul: Uh, what time do you have?

Mary: 3:00. Why?

Paul: I've got to go to class.

Mary: Oh, I'm sorry to hear that. I wanted to talk more. Well . . . have a good class!

Paul: Thanks. See you later

2. A boy is describing his day to his father.

Father: How was your day Billy?

Billy: Pretty good.

Father: What'd you do?

Billy: Well, in the morning I went on a hike with Tommy and Joey.

Father: How was that?

Billy: It was pretty good. When we got out in the woods, we saw a deer.

Father: Really? How big was it?

Billy: It was gigantic! (*pause*) Unfortunately, it ran away.

Father: And then what did you do?

Billy: We went swimming in Miller Lake.

Father: That must have been wonderful on a hot day like today!

Billy: Yeah, it was.

Father: What's Miller Lake like nowadays?

Billy: Well, let me think, (*pause*), uh, it's really deep and has an island in the middle of it. It's surrounded by woods.

Father: It sounds the same as when I was a boy! (*pause*) So what did you do after that?

Billy: Well, then it started to rain!

Father: That's too bad. What did you do when it started to rain?

Billy: We ran to that old deserted house on Forest Road. The pink one where the Smiths used to live.

Father: Were you able to get in?

Billy: Yeah. We stayed there until the rain stopped and then came back home.

Father: So, it sounds like you had an adventurous day.

Billy: I guess so. How was your day?

Father: Well, I just did paperwork all day.

Billy: Sounds boring!

Father: It was. (*pause*) Well, enjoy your youth son. It'll pass very quickly.

Billy: I'll try Dad. (*pause*) Well, I have to go do some math homework.

Father: I'll see you at dinner.

Billy: O.K.

CHAPTER FOUR

ENDING A CONVERSATION

LISTENING

Look at the picture. The woman is trying to end the conversation. What do you think she should say?

Listen to each dialogue and fill in the blanks with T (true) or F (false). Listen again to check your answers.

1. Amy has to go home to study.

_____ Amy wants to continue the conversation.

_____ Amy's uncle is now in the hospital.

_____ Amy is studying computer science, English, and biology.

_____ John wants to continue the conversation.

2. Pon and Fyodor are talking. Pon has to go home.

_____ Pon has to leave because he feels that it's late.

_____ Fyodor will probably see Ms. Kim tomorrow.

_____ It is probably Friday.

3. Mary and Susan are talking. Mary is going home after a visit to the city.

_____ Susan wants Mary to write a postcard.

_____ The two women met by chance the day before.

_____ Mary won't ever see Susan again.

FROM THE DIALOGUES

There are many possible ways to end a conversation. Generally, people use a variety of expressions to end the conversation __gradually__. Study the vocabulary.

PRE-CLOSINGS

These expressions give the idea, "I will be leaving soon."

I'm so glad I ran into you yesterday. (ran into = met unexpectedly)
Oh! **What time do you have, Pon?**
I didn't realize that it was that late. **I guess that I'd better be going.**
Well, **it was really nice talking to you** again.
But **listen, we'll have to get together** again sometime.
Well, **I'd better get on. I'll give you a call** when I get home.
Well, **it's been nice talking to you,** John.
Well, **I'd better be going now.** I've got a lot of homework tonight!
I'm sorry, but I've really got to go now. It's starting to get late.
It was wonderful seeing you again.
I'll probably see you tomorrow.

MESSAGE FOR SOMEONE

Say hello to Hsing Yi **for me**, will you?
And **if you see** Ms. Kim, **tell her** to give me a call.
Say hello to Harry.

GOOD WISHES FOR THE FUTURE

Have a good weekend.
Have a nice trip.
Well, **take care,** Mary, **and don't forget to send us a postcard.**

CLOSINGS

Bye.
See you next August.
Good-bye
I'll see you around.
Well, **good night,** John.

CONVERSATION PRACTICE

1. Turn to page 42 and read each dialogue in pairs. Ask your teacher to explain any grammar or vocabulary that you do not understand.

VOCABULARY EXPANSION
Study the additional vocabulary.
PRE-CLOSINGS
Thanks for inviting me tonight.
MESSAGE FOR SOMEONE
Give my best to _____!
GOOD WISHES FOR THE FUTURE
Enjoy yourself!
Good Luck!
Bon Voyage!
CLOSINGS
So long!

*2. Put a **P** in front of any sentence which is a Pre-closing. Put an **M** in front of any sentence which is a Message for Someone. Put a **W** in front of a sentence which is a Good Wish for the Future. Put a **C** in front of any sentence which is a Closing. Put an **X** in front of any other sentences.*

_____ It's been nice talking to you.

_____ See you tomorrow.

_____ What's up?

_____ Say hello to Tom.

_____ Have a nice trip!

_____ I saw a great movie last night!

_____ So long.

_____ It's really late!

_____ Give my best to your family.

_____ We'll have to get together again.

_____ Hmmmm, let me see.

3. *In pairs, read the conversations and write an ending for each. Then read the completed conversations to the class.*

1. A: Hi, Martin! How're you doing?

   B: Pretty good, I love my classes!

   A: What're you taking?

   B: Physics, biology, and chemistry.

   A: That sounds difficult!

   B: Well, I have to take a lot of science to be a doctor. What're you taking?

   A: Uh, I have tennis and American history.

   B: What's your major?

   A: I haven't decided yet. I may go into business.
      (*end the conversation*)

   _____

   _____

   _____

2. A: Hazel! It's so nice to see you. How have you been?

   B: Not bad, and you?

   A: I've been doing pretty well, thanks. Say, how's Madge?

   B: She's doing much better thanks. The doctor says that she'll be back to normal in a couple of weeks.

   A: I'm glad to hear that.

   B: And how's little Billy?

   A: You wouldn't believe how big he is! He's in fifth grade already!

   B: I'd love to see him sometime.
      (*end the conversation*)

   _____

   _____

   _____

3. A: Hi, Sally. Did you have a nice weekend?

   B: Yeah, I went to San Francisco with some friends.

   A: Really? What did you do there?

   B: We went to a disco Friday night, and then we went for a drive over the Golden Gate Bridge.

   A: That sounds great! I just stayed home and studied for the big test.

   B: That's too bad.

   A: Yeah, it was really boring.

   B: What did you do on Sunday?

   A: More of the same. I just stayed home and studied.

   (*end the conversation*)

   _____

   _____

   _____

4. *Put the conversation in the correct order by numbering the sentences. When you finish, compare your answers with a classmate's answers.*

   _____ Well, it was really nice talking to you.

   _____ O.K., see you.

   _____ Yeah, I'm really glad that we ran into each other.

   _____ Yes, you'd better get going. The airport traffic can be terrible!

   _____ Bye!

   _____ I'll give you a call.

   __1__ Oh, it's already three o'clock! I'd better be going! I've got to be at the airport at four.

   _____ Me too. We'll have to get together again sometime.

YOUR TURN

1. Survey

Ask five members of your class for the information in the chart below. Be sure to introduce yourself (**Hi, I'm** _____) and use an opener (**May I ask you a few questions?**). When you finish, use pre-closings and closings to end the conversation smoothly.

Name?	What classes are you taking?	Do you have any hobbies? What are they?	What is your favorite sport?
1.			
2.			
3.			
4.			
5.			

ENDING A CONVERSATION TRANSCRIPT

1. Amy has to go home to study.

Amy: Well, it's been nice talking to you John.

John: Hey, Amy, I forgot to ask you about your uncle.

Amy: Uh, he's doing much better now. He came home from the hospital last week.

John: I'm glad to hear that.

Amy: Well, I'd better be going now, I've got a lot of homework tonight!

John: What classes are you taking?

Amy: Let's see . . . computer science, English, and math.

John: Me too. Who's your English professor?

Amy: I'm sorry, but I've really got to go now. It's starting to get late.

John: That's too bad. We'll have to get together sometime. I'd really love to talk more.

Amy: Well, I've been really busy lately, but maybe after the term's over.

John: Sounds great!

Amy: I'll see you around!

John: I'll probably see you tomorrow.

Amy: Yeah. Well, good night John.

John: Good night, Amy!

2. Pon and Fyodor are talking. Pon has to go home.

Pon: Oh!! What time do you have, Fyodor?

Fyodor: It's almost five.

Pon: I didn't realize that it was that late. I guess that I'd better get going. Hsing Yi gets home at six.

Fyodor: Well, it was really nice talking to you again.

Pon: I feel the same way. But listen, we'll have to get together again sometime.

Fyodor: Say hello to Hsing Yi for me, will you?

Pon: I'll do that!

Fyodor: And if you see Ms. Kim, tell her to give me a call.

Pon: I'll probably see her the day after tomorrow.

Fyodor: Have a good weekend.

Pon: You too.

Fyodor: Bye.

3. Mary and Susan are talking. Mary is going home after a visit to the city.

Mary: . . . and then she said that it wasn't a good idea for me to come to Chicago!

Susan: Is that your bus coming?

Mary: It looks like it.

Susan: Well, take care, Mary, and don't forget to send us a postcard.

Mary: I won't. It was wonderful seeing you again!

Susan: I'm so glad that I ran into you yesterday.

Mary: Me too. Say hello to Harry.

Susan: I will.

Mary: Well, I'd better get on. I'll give you a call when I get home.

Susan: Good idea. Have a nice trip!

Mary: I'll try. See you next August.

Susan: I'm looking forward to it.

Mary: Good-bye.

Susan: Good-bye.

REVIEW OF CHAPTERS 1–4

SCRAMBLED CONVERSATIONS

Put the conversations in the correct order by numbering the sentences. When you finish, compare your answers with a classmate's answers.

1. *June runs into Lee in a supermarket.*

_____ Well, actually, we'll be pretty busy with moving in for a while .

__1__ Lee! I didn't expect to see you here. Don't you live over near the beach?

_____ Hey, we'll have to get together sometime.

_____ Well, when you have time, give me a call.

_____ I'll do that. Bye.

_____ That's wonderful! We'll be neighbors.

_____ Yeah, I guess we will. Well, I'd better be going. I have a lot of things to buy.

_____ Bye.

_____ Well, actually Mary and I just moved over here.

2. *May and Jonathan meet in their university library.*

_____ Really? That's wonderful! Congratulations!

_____ We should get together before you graduate.

_____ I'm fine, Jonathan, but I'm tired from too much studying. How've *you* been?

_____ Bye.

_____ That sounds great. Why don't you give me a call?

_____ I've been really busy with school too. I study all day and every night. I'm going to graduate in June.

__1__ Hi May. How are you?

_____ O.K. I will.

_____ Thanks. I've worked really hard to do it. Well, I'd better get back to studying if I want to finish in June.

MATCHING

Match the sentences in Column One with the sentences in Column Two.

Column One

_____ What's up?

_____ My dog was hit by a car yesterday.

_____ What was it like?

_____ Don't forget to write!

_____ Did you say five-oh or one-five?

_____ How did you like it?

_____ Well, it was nice talking to you.

_____ What time is the flight?

_____ Joe, I'd like you to meet Sally.

_____ Have a good weekend!

Column Two

a. I said five-oh.

b. Nice to meet you.

c. I'm sorry to hear that.

d. Nothing much.

e. I won't.

f. It's at 4:30 in the afternoon.

g. I'll try.

h. We'll have to get together again sometime.

i. It was beautiful!

j. I liked it very much!

REMEMBER

1. If you don't understand something, ask a question. (*Could you repeat that?*)

2. If you do understand, say something to show that you understand.
   (*Uh-huh, Really?, How nice!*)

3. If you need time to think, use an appropriate expression.
   (*Hmmm, Let me think, Well . . .*)

4. Avoid silence. (5 seconds is too much)

5. Give complete responses to questions, not only *yes* or *no*.

6. Ask open questions. (*How did you like _____? What's _____ like?*)

CONVERSATION MAZE ONE

CONVERSATION MAZE ONE

Read the section marked *Situation*. Ask your teacher to explain any vocabulary or grammar you do not understand. Then, read the question and choose one of the possible answers (*A, B,* or *C*). Each answer will send you to a new numbered section. Go to the number indicated and read the *Explanation*. If you choose the best answer, the *Situation* will continue and another question will be asked. If you did not choose the best answer, you will be instructed to return to the previous section and try again. Continue through the maze until you have ended the conversation.

When you are reading one section, you may **not** look at any other section.

SITUATION

You are Juan, an exchange student from the city of Merida in Mexico. You have been in the United States for 3 months studying English. You have been invited to a party at the apartment of Kaoru, a fellow student. You arrive at the party, but you don't see anyone you know. After a few moments, a young woman approaches you and says, "Hello, I'm Pam."

What should you say?

    A. Hi, I'm Juan. I'm a friend of Kaoru's from school. ➡ Go to **32.**

    B. Hi, I'm Juan. ➡ Go to **19.**

    C. Hi, I'm Juan. Do you like skiing? ➡ Go to **5.**

---

1 **EXPLANATION:** This is not the best response because the information is not very interesting. ➡ Return to 18.

---

2 **EXPLANATION:** This is the best response because it concentrates on what Pam does not understand—*Mayan* and *ruins*. She already understands *beaches*.

Pam says, "Oh, really? I don't know anything about them."

What do you say?

    A. Didn't you study them in school? ➡ Go to **29.**

    B. Hmmm . . . well, they were an ancient people who were basically peaceful. They were very advanced in astronomy and mathematics. ➡ Go to **16.**

    C. They were very interesting. They had a very advanced culture which lasted a long time. ➡ Go to **11.**

---

3 **EXPLANATION:** For this situation, you need a more enthusiastic response to the word *beautiful*. ➡ Return to 34.

---

4 **EXPLANATION:** This is a good specific clarification question. It shows that you know that *Vail* is a kind of place.

Pam says, "Actually, it's a city with a lot of ski resorts."

You want to encourage Pam to continue. What's the best response?

    A. I see. ➡ Go to **34.**

    B. Hmmm . . . ➡ Go to **30.**

    C. That's too bad! ➡ Go to **20.**

---

5 **EXPLANATION:** This is incorrect because it is too abrupt. People who have just met usually talk about personal information. ➡ Return to the **beginning situation**.

6 **EXPLANATION:** This is much too short. You should give a complete answer. ➡ Return to 32.

7 **EXPLANATION:** This is correct because Pam's statement is a pre-closing. She wants to end the conversation.

Pam says, "I'll talk to you again later. Bye." (*Pam moves off toward the kitchen.*)

8 **EXPLANATION:** This is best because it is a continuation of the previous topic, personal information.

Pam says, "Oh, I'm from Erie, Pennsylvania originally, but I've lived here in Denver for three years now."

What can you say?

        A. How do you like it here? ➡ Go to **31**.

        B. Do you like Denver? ➡ Go to **23**.

        C. Oh, really! I went to Pennsylvania three years ago. ➡ Go to **15**.

9 **EXPLANATION:** This is not the best answer because it only repeats; it does not explain. ➡ Return to **26**.

10 **EXPLANATION:** Pam is trying to *end* the conversation. This response would *begin a new topic*. ➡ Return to **24**.

11 **EXPLANATION:** This information is too vague. ➡ Return to **2**.

12 **EXPLANATION:** This is incorrect because *What's it like?* does not mean *What do you like?* It means *Please describe it to me*. ➡ Return to **18**.

13 **EXPLANATION:** You need an *enthusiastic* response here, not a sympathetic one. ➡ Return to **34**.

14 **EXPLANATION:** This is not the best answer because it does not focus on what was not understood —*Mayan ruins*. The information about *beaches* is not relevant. ➡ Return to **26**.

15 **EXPLANATION:** You want to discuss *her* personal information, *not yours*. ➡ Return to **8**.

16 **EXPLANATION:** This answer is best because it gives a good summary of the most important information about the *Mayas*.

Pam continues, "I'd love to see the pyramids".
You reply, "Well, if you ever go to Mexico, please call my family. They'd be glad to help you."
Pam says, "I'll do that." (*pause*)

You feel that you have told Pam a great deal about yourself. Now, you would like some information about her. What can you say?

        A. What kind of movies do you like? ➡ Go to **33**.

        B. What kind of person are you? ➡ Go to **25**.

        C. Where are you from? ➡ Go to **8**.

17 **EXPLANATION:** An open question would be better. ➡ Return to **31**.

18 EXPLANATION: This is the best response because it is complete and gives personal information.

Pam says, "I've never been to the Yucatan. What's it like?"

**You want to think for a moment and give a good answer.
What do you say?**

> A. Hmmm . . . well, it's a peninsula, so there is a lot of water and it's near Guatemala. ➠ Go to **1**.

> B. Well . . . let me see, it's very tropical. Most people go there to see the beaches and the Mayan ruins. ➠ Go to **26**.

> C. Hmmm . . . well, I like to swim and listen to music. ➠ Go to **12**.

19 EXPLANATION: This is incorrect because it is too short. It does not help the conversation develop. ➠ Return to the **beginning situation**.

20 EXPLANATION: That's too bad! is for sad news. ➠ Return to **4**.

21 EXPLANATION: Your parents are irrelevant to this conversation. ➠ Return to **31**.

22 EXPLANATION: Another good opinion/open question.

Pam says, "Personally, I prefer Vail because of the good snow and beautiful scenery".

You do not know what Vail is. What is the best question?

> A. Is Vail a ski resort? ➠ Go to **4**.

> B. Could you repeat that? ➠ Go to **35**.

> C. Vail? ➠ Go to **27**.

23 EXPLANATION: You should rephrase this as an open question. ➠ Return to **8**.

24 EXPLANATION: This situation needs an enthusiastic response to the word *beautiful*, so this is the best response.

Pam says, "It was. . . . Well, I need to get something to drink."

What should you say?

> A. Do you mind if I go with you? We can continue our conversation. ➠ Go to **36**.

> B. It was nice talking to you Pam. ➠ Go to **7**.

> C. By the way, what would you like to drink? ➠ Go to **10**.

25 EXPLANATION: This is much too personal. ➠ Return to **16**.

26 EXPLANATION: This is best because it gives information about things that are relevant to a visitor—*beaches* and *ruins*.

Pam says, "The beaches and the what?" (*She looks confused.*)

What do you say?

> A. The beaches and the Mayan ruins. ➠ Go to **9**.

> B. The beaches on the ocean are very beautiful and there are also many old buildings. ➠ Go to **14**.

> C. The Mayan ruins. The Mayans were a people who built a lot of stone pyramids and other buildings. You can still see parts of the buildings. ➠ Go to **2**.

27 EXPLANATION: Try to make a clarification question as specific as possible. ➙ Return to **22**.

28 EXPLANATION: This is not the best response because it gives obvious information. You need some new information here. ➙ Return to **32**.

29 EXPLANATION: This is rather impolite because it could imply that Pam was not well educated. ➙ Return to **2**.

30 EXPLANATION: *Hmmm . . .* does not encourage. It shows that you are thinking. ➙ Return to **4**.

31 EXPLANATION: This is a good open question.

Pam says, "I really love it! I love to ski and walk in the mountains."

What is the best response?

        A. My parents always loved skiing. ➙ Go to **21**.

        B. Really? What's your favorite ski resort? ➙ Go to **22**.

        C. Colorado is a great place to go skiing, isn't it? ➙ Go to **17**.

32 EXPLANATION: This is the best response because it identifies you and gives the listener something to comment on—*school*.

Pam says, "Oh, really? Then you're a foreign student?"

What should you say?

        A. Yes, I am. ➙ Go to **6**.

        B. Yes, I'm studying English. ➙ Go to **28**.

        C. Yes, I'm from the Yucatan, in Mexico. I live in Merida, the capital of the province. ➙ Go to **18**.

33 EXPLANATION: This is a very abrupt change of topic. You should continue talking about personal information. ➙ Return to **16**.

34 EXPLANATION: This is good because it is neutral encouragement.

Pam says, "I just came back from there yesterday. It had just snowed, so everything was beautiful!"

What can you say?

        A. Uh-huh. ➙ Go to **3**.

        B. That must have been difficult. ➙ Go to **13**.

        C. It sounds wonderful! ➙ Go to **24**.

35 EXPLANATION: This clarification is too general. It does not tell the speaker what was not understood. ➙ Return to **22**.

36 EXPLANATION: Pam used a pre-closing to show that she wants to end the conversation. She does not want to *continue* the conversation. ➙ Return to **24**.

CHAPTER FIVE

WEEKENDS

LISTENING

Look at the pictures. The people are thinking about the things they did last weekend, and the things they plan to do next weekend. What activities did you do last weekend? What activities do you plan to do next weekend?

Listen to each dialogue and fill in the blanks with T (true) or F (false). Listen again to check your answers.

1. *Patsy and Mark meet on Monday morning.*

_____ Patsy had an exciting weekend.

_____ Mark went to the beach and then went dancing.

_____ Patsy went to a Chinese restaurant.

I worked out in my gym.

I'm going fishing with my cousins.

2. *David and Ken meet on Friday afternoon.*

_____ Ken is invited to go skiing with some friends.

_____ Ken has already agreed to go fishing with his cousins.

_____ Ken's friends are going fishing again in two weeks.

_____ Ken's brother will be able to go skiing with the group.

FROM THE DIALOGUES

Study the vocabulary.

TALKING ABOUT LAST WEEKEND (PAST)

> **NOTE:** On Monday, some people may use the word *this* to talk about the past weekend. e.g., "What *did* you do *this* weekend?"

General Questions	Possible Answers
How was your weekend?	Fine, thanks.
What did you do?	I stayed home and read.
Did you have a nice weekend?	Yeah, I went to the beach on Saturday.

TALKING ABOUT NEXT WEEKEND (FUTURE)

General Question	Possible Answers
What's your brother **going to do this weekend?**	**He's going to** drive to Brooksville to see his girlfriend.
What are you going to do this weekend?	**I'm planning to** go fishing with my cousins.

> **NOTE:** In normal conversation, we do not say *I will* do something next weekend.
> We say: *I'm going to . . . ; I'm planning to. . . ; I want to . . . ;* or *I'd like to. . . .*
> Do <u>not</u> say *I have a plan to . . .*

ACTIVITIES WITH GO

go to the beach
go dancing
go out (on a date)
go out to eat
go to a movie
go skiing
go fishing

OTHER ACTIVITIES

stay home
read a book
watch TV
work out (in a gym)
drive to (place)

CONVERSATION PRACTICE

1. Turn to page 60 and read each dialogue in pairs. Ask your teacher to explain any grammar or vocabulary that you do not understand.

VOCABULARY EXPANSION

Study the additional vocabulary.

TALKING ABOUT NEXT WEEKEND

I want to go visit my sister.
I'd like to go swimming.

> **NOTE:** Be careful with *I'd* like to . . . (future) and *I like to* . . . (habitual)

ACTIVITIES WITH *GO*

go camping	go shopping	go to school
go driving/go for a drive	go sightseeing	go to see someone
go for a bicycle ride	go swimming	go to work
go hiking	go to church	go visit someone
go home		

OTHER ACTIVITIES

call someone (on the phone)	take a nap	watch a video
listen to music	visit a museum	write a letter
sleep late		

SPORTS AND GAMES: ACTIVITIES WITH *PLAY*

Team Sports	Individual Sports	Games
baseball	golf	chess
football	tennis	checkers
soccer	racquetball	backgammon
basketball	ping pong	(playing) cards
volleybal		

2. In pairs, rate the following weekend activities from 1 to 5 (1 = excellent; 5 = terrible). When you finish, compare your answers with your classmate's answers.

This weekend I'm going to . . .

_____ go camping.

_____ go for a drive.

_____ play an individual sport (such as tennis).

_____ sleep late.

_____ watch TV.

_____ go fishing.

_____ go to a movie.

_____ go shopping.

_____ read a book/magazine.

_____ listen to music.

_____ play a team sport (such as softball).

_____ take a nap.

_____ go for a bicycle ride.

_____ play a game (such as chess).

_____ eat/cook.

_____ visit a museum.

_____ other: _____

_____ other: _____

3. Put the conversation in the correct order by numbering the sentences. When you finish, compare your answers with a classmate's answers.

_____ I'm doing pretty well thanks.

_____ It was! I'm going to go back this weekend. Do you want to come?

_____ What'd you do?

_____ Did you have a nice weekend?

_____ How was the snow?

__1__ Hi Jane, how're you doing?

_____ It sounds wonderful.

_____ It was nearly perfect. It had just snowed the night before, so there was no ice.

_____ I'd love to.

_____ Fine thanks. And you?

_____ Yeah, I had a great time.

_____ I went skiing.

YOUR TURN

1. Last Weekend

*Write down four things that you did last weekend. Remember to use the past tense. Then, tell a partner the four things you did. The listener must respond to the speaker, using listener expressions (**Really! That must have been interesting! That's too bad!**).*

1. I went _____

_____

2. _____

_____

3. _____

_____

4. _____

_____

I went skiing.

That's too bad!

2. Next Weekend

*Write down four things that you are going to do or want to do next weekend. Then tell a partner about your weekend. The listener must respond to the speaker, using listener expressions (**Really! That must have been interesting! That's too bad!**).*

1. I'd like to _____

_____

2. I am planning to _____

_____

3. I'm going to _____

_____

4. _____

_____

3. Any Weekend

Write down four things that you like to do on weekends.

1. I like to _____

   _____

2. I enjoy (verb + *-ing*) _____

   _____

3. _____

   _____

4. _____

   _____

5. Survey

Ask five members of your class for the information in the chart below. When you finish, compare your list with your classmates' lists. What activities are the most popular?

Find someone who _____ last weekend.

Activity	Name (s)
went dancing	
wrote a letter	
went for a bicycle ride	
took a nap	
listened to music	
other:	

Find someone who is going to _____ next weekend.

Activity	Name (s)
go to work	
play tennis	
work out in a gym	
go visit someone	
play soccer	
other:	

WEEKENDS TRANSCRIPT

1. Patsy and Mark meet on Monday morning.

Mark: Hi Patsy, how're you doing?

Patsy: Fine, thanks and you?

Mark: Not bad. How was your weekend?

Patsy: Pretty boring.

Mark: What did you do?

Patsy: I just stayed home and read some books for a research paper I have to write for history class.

Mark: That's too bad. Did you do anything else?

Patsy: Well, on Sunday, I watched TV.

Mark: Uh-huh.

Patsy: Did you have a nice weekend?

Mark: Yeah, I went to the beach on Saturday and then Saturday night I went dancing with my girlfriend Carol.

Patsy: That must have been fun!

Mark: Yes it was. And on Sunday, I worked out in my gym and then went out on a date with Carol again.

Patsy: Where did you go?

Mark: We went out to eat at that new Chinese restaurant and then went to a movie.

Patsy: Sounds fun.

Mark: Well listen, I've got to go.

Patsy: O.K. I'll see you later.

Mark: Sure.

Patsy: Bye.

2. David and Ken meet on Friday afternoon.

David: Hey, Ken. Wait up!

Ken: Hi David. What's up?

David: Uh . . . Bob and Terry and I are going skiing this weekend and we wanted to know if you'd want to come, too.

Ken: I'd really like to, but I'm planning to go fishing with my cousins.

David: That's too bad, but we'll be going again in two weeks!

Ken: Great! I'll go with you then.

David: Hey, what's your brother going to do this weekend?

Ken: He's going to drive to Brooksville to see his girlfriend.

David: Oh, well. Maybe he can come some other time.

Ken: Yeah. (*pause*) Well, I guess I'd better be going.

David: I'll give you a call sometime next week.

Ken: O.K., see you.

David: Good-bye.

CHAPTER SIX

WEATHER

LISTENING

Look at the pictures. The weather can be very severe in some parts of the world. What is the weather like in your country?

Listen to each dialogue and fill in the blanks with a T (true) or F (false). Listen again to check your answers.

1. Two women are standing at a bus stop.

_____ It is December.

_____ One of the women was planning to go for a drive with her husband.

_____ One woman is going to the coast to visit friends.

2. Two friends meet at the beach.

_____ Abdul and Carlos meet accidentally.

_____ The temperature is 90 degrees.

_____ Abdul likes the humidity.

_____ Carlos lives on the coast of Peru.

_____ There is sometimes strong wind in Saudi Arabia.

3. You are listening to a national weather announcement on the telephone.

_____ The date is March 15.

_____ It will be foggy in the morning.

_____ The early afternoon will be clear.

_____ After 3 or 4 o'clock it will begin to rain.

_____ It will be extremely windy tomorrow.

_____ Tomorrow will be colder than today.

FROM THE DIALOGUES

Study the vocabulary.

TALKING ABOUT WEATHER

<u>Description Question</u>

What's the winter **like** in your mountains?

What's the weather like?

**What's the weather going to be
like tomorrow?**

<u>Possible Answer</u>

There's snow everywhere.

It gets cold in the desert.
(*gets = becomes*)
In Peru, **it's very** humid on the coast.
In the mountains, **it's much** drier.

The temperature will be **in the
(upper, mid, low) (90s, 80s, . . .).**
There is a 30% chance of rain
A cold front is moving in.

OTHER STATEMENTS ABOUT THE WEATHER

The weatherman / weatherwoman said (that) it was going to rain tomorrow.
I don't mind the heat.
This humidity **is killing me!**

WAYS TO DESCRIBE WEATHER

(freezing) cold	**(burning) hot**
cool/cooler	**warm/warming up**
foggy	**clear/clearing up**
(partly) cloudy	**sunny**
humid	**dry/drier**
95 degrees	**beautiful**

WEATHER CONDITIONS

heat	**(moderate) wind**
snow	**a (wind) storm**
rain	**a cold/warm front**
scattered showers	

GEOGRAPHICAL DESCRIPTIONS / SEASONS

GEOGRAPHICAL DESCRIPTIONS	SEASONS
in the desert	**winter**
in the mountains	**spring**
on the coast	**summer**
inland	**fall (autumn)**
next to a lake	**wet**
near a river	**dry**
	monsoon

CONVERSATION PRACTICE

1. Turn to page 68 and read each dialogue in pairs. Take turns reading dialogue 3 to each other. Ask your teacher to explain any grammar or vocabulary that you do not understand.

2. Put the conversations in the correct order by numbering the sentences. When you finish, compare your answers with a classmate's answers.

1. _____ I heard on the radio that the storm should clear up by 8:00 tonight.

   _____ Certainly, Ms. Baker. Cream and sugar?

   _____ Good morning Harry. How are you ?

   _____ I am too, except it's so good for the plants. The parks were looking awfully brown for a while!

   _____ That would be wonderful!

   __1__ Good morning, Ms. Baker.

   _____ Yes, it would. (*pause*) Harry, could you get me a cup of coffee?

   _____ Please.

   _____ Not bad, but I certainly am tired of rain!

   _____ Yes they were. Still, I was hoping to go to the beach with my girlfriend.

It will be cooler tomorrow.

2. _____ The weatherlady said it would be cooler tomorrow.

   _____ Well, then I'll see you tomorrow.

   _____ I know what you mean! I can hardly stand it.

   __1__ Good afternoon, Joe.

   _____ O.K. I guess. I'd be better if it wasn't so hot!

   _____ I hope she's right! It certainly is unusually hot for this time of year.

   _____ Oh, hi Max. How're you doing?

   _____ Well, I'd better be going home now; Lucille wants me to cook a chicken for dinner.

YOUR TURN

1. Describe the Weather

Briefly describe your city's weather, using the questions as a guide. When you finish, read your description to the class.

Where is your city? (on the coast, inland, in the mountains, etc.)

How far is it from the equator/North Pole?

How many seasons are there?

How much rainfall does it get?

What is the coldest time of year? the hottest?

Is it sunny, cloudy, windy, etc.?

How cold does it get?

How hot does it get?

_____

_____

_____

_____

2. Weather Expressions

In pairs, read the following weather expressions and try to guess the meaning of each. Write down your answers. Then compare your answers with your classmate's answers.

1. It's raining cats and dogs!

_____

_____

_____

2. It's good weather for ducks.

_____

_____

_____

3. I wouldn't send a dog out on a night like this!

_____

_____

_____

4. "Everyone always talks about the weather, but nobody ever does anything about it!" (Mark Twain)

_____

_____

_____

5. It's coming down in buckets!

_____

_____

_____

6. Red sky at night, sailors' delight; red sky at morning, sailors take warning.

_____

_____

_____

3. *Make a list of weather expressions from your country. Compare your list with your classmate's lists. How are they different from the expressions in English?*

4. Survey

Ask five members of your class for the information in the chart below. When you finish, compare your list with your classmates' lists.

Name	What's the weather like in your hometown?	What's your favorite kind of weather?	What's your least favorite kind of weather?	What's your favorite season?
1.				
2.				
3.				
4.				
5.				

WEATHER TRANSCRIPT

1. Two women are standing at a bus stop.

Woman 1: It's a little cold today, isn't it?

Woman 2: Yeah, it is. I was hoping that it would warm up.

Woman 1: I know what you mean. I thought that by April the temperature would be in the 70s.

Woman 2: The weatherman said that it was going to rain tomorrow.

Woman 1: That's terrible. I was planning to drive to the coast with my husband.

Woman 2: Yeah. I was going to visit some friends in the mountains, but I changed my mind. I'm staying home where it's warm.

Woman 1: Well, here's my bus. It was nice talking to you.

Woman 2: Bye.

2. Two friends meet at the beach.

Carlos: Abdul, I'm over here.

Abdul: I'm glad I found you Carlos. Where are the others?

Carlos: I guess they haven't gotten here yet. (*pause*) It's a great day for the beach. It's so sunny and beautiful.

Abdul: Yeah, but I can't believe how humid it is here!

Carlos: And hot! The weatherman said that it was 95 degrees!

Abdul: I don't mind the heat. In Saudi Arabia we have plenty of heat, but it's dry there. This humidity is killing me!

Carlos: In Peru, it's very humid on the coast, but up where I live in the mountains, it's much drier.

Abdul: Really?

Carlos: Yeah, it's never this humid and it's always much cooler. I've never felt heat like this!

Abdul: What's the winter like in the mountains?

Carlos: It's freezing cold. There's snow everywhere.

Abdul: It gets cold in the desert in Saudi Arabia, but on the coast it's not bad. The wind can be a real problem though.

Carlos: The wind?

Abdul: During the windstorms, sand is blown into everything.

Carlos: Oh! I think that I see the others. Let's walk over there.

Abdul: Good idea.

3. A recorded National Weather announcement on the telephone.

Weatherlady: The following is a forecast of the National Weather Service issued at Gainesville for May 15. In the morning, it will be foggy, clearing up slightly by noon. The early afternoon will be partly cloudy clearing by 3 or 4. There is a 30% chance of rain in the early morning. Temperatures will be in the low 70s until tomorrow when a cold front moving in from the north will bring scattered showers, moderate wind, and temperatures in the low 40s.

CHAPTER SEVEN

MUSIC

LISTENING

Look at the picture. Can you name some of the different musicians and instruments in it?

Listen to the dialogue and fill in the blanks with T (true) or F (false). Listen again to check your answers.

Tom and Amy have just met at a party.

_____ Tom is from New York.

_____ The party is in Texas.

_____ The music at the party is a band called the *Talking Feet*.

_____ The *Talking Feet's* music has a strong beat.

_____ The *Talking Feet* are from Las Vegas.

_____ Tom and Amy both like the words of the songs.

_____ The party music is classical.

_____ Tom likes jazz from the Sixties.

_____ Tom and Amy both like the Miles Parker Quintet.

_____ In Florida, many people listen to the blues.

_____ Sonny Franklin is a blues musician.

_____ Sonny Franklin's wife is named Diamond Tooth Mary Macrae.

_____ Mary Macrae is a singer.

_____ Amy and Tom both like Mozart and Beethoven.

_____ Tom really loves Bach.

_____ Amy needs to talk to a friend who just arrived.

FROM THE DIALOGUES

Study the vocabulary.

TALKING ABOUT MUSIC	PREFERENCE OR OPINION

General Questions
What's this music?

What kind of music do you like?
Do you ever listen to classical music?

Do you know Miles Parker?

Opinion Question
What do you think about Bach?

Statements
We listen to the blues a lot.
I listen to a lot of jazz **from
(the Fifties, the Sixties, . . .)**

Possible Preference / Opinion
It's the Talking Feet. **They're
really popular now.**
Spanish guitar and jazz.
I'm crazy about Mozart and
Beethoven.
I love his Quintet.

Possible Preference / Opinion
I prefer Beethoven **to** Bach.

MORE PREFERENCES AND OPINIONS ABOUT MUSIC

Their lyrics **are really** interesting. (lyrics = words)
Actually, **I don't usually listen to** such modern music.
Her **voice** is still really strong.
I've never heard of them. (I don't know them.)

TYPES OF POPULAR MUSIC IN THE UNITED STATES

the blues
classical
jazz

MUSIC PEOPLE

composer = person who writes the music
saxophone player
guitarist

MUSIC GROUPINGS

band
orchestra
quintet

PARTS OF MUSIC

rhythm (beat)
lyrics (words)

ADJECTIVES FOR MUSIC

acoustic	**popular**
interesting	**romantic**
modern	**soothing**
poetic	

CONVERSATION PRACTICE

1. Turn to page 78 and read the dialogue in pairs. Ask your teacher to explain any vocabulary or grammar you do not understand.

VOCABULARY EXPANSION

Study the additional vocabulary.

TYPES OF POPULAR MUSIC IN THE UNITED STATES

big band	hiphop	rap
bluegrass	heavy metal	ragtime
country and western	marches	reggae
disco	new age	rock 'n' roll
easy listening	oldies	samba
folk	pop	salsa

MUSIC PEOPLE

musician	pianist
songwriter	singer

MUSIC GROUPINGS

solo	quartet
trio	group

PARTS OF MUSIC

harmony
melody

ADJECTIVES FOR MUSIC

beautiful	electric/electronic	simple
boring	fast	slow
complicated	loud	soft
disturbing	noisy	traditional
dramatic	peaceful	unpopular
dynamic	pretty	vocal

2. *Fill in the blanks with words from the list.*

quintet	lyrics	acoustic	soothing	romantic	orchestra	rhythm	modern

1. I don't really like electric instruments. I like _____ instruments.

2. The words of a song are the _____.

3. Five musicians together are a _____.

4. I prefer traditional music to _____ music.

5. I don't like music which makes me nervous. I prefer _____ music.

6. An _____ is a very large group of musicians.

7. In rock n' roll, the _____ section is usually a drummer and a bass player.

8. I listen to very _____ music because love and other emotions are important to me.

3. *Match the adjectives in Column One with their opposites in Column Two.*

Column One

_____ soft

_____ peaceful

_____ simple

_____ acoustic

_____ interesting

Column Two

a. noisy

b. boring

c. loud

d. electric

e. complicated

4. *Put the conversation in the correct order by numbering the sentences. When you finish, compare your answers with your classmate's answers.*

_____ What kind of music do you listen to then?

_____ Because it's so loud and it has a heavy beat.

_____ Jazz? How come?

_____ I really like heavy metal.

_____ Because I want music to relax me.

_____ I listen to jazz and classical.

__1__ What kind of music do you like?

_____ Really? Why do you like heavy metal?

_____ Really! I hate loud music.

YOUR TURN

1. Musical Likes and Dislikes

In pairs, fill in the blanks. Then tell your partner your answers. The listener must respond to the speaker, using listener expressions and an opinion/preference.

Examples: A: I really love pop music.
B: Oh? I prefer rock n' roll to pop music.

A: I really love pop music.
B: Me too. I'm crazy about Janet Jackson.

1. I really love _____.

2. I really hate _____.

3. I usually listen to _____.

4. My favorite kind of music is _____.

5. Lately I have been listening to _____.

6. I prefer _____ to _____.

7. I like _____ better than _____.

2. Interview

In pairs, interview a partner using the questions below. Ask for reasons for each of your partner's answers.

Interview Questions

Do you prefer electric or acoustic musical instruments?
Do you prefer loud or soft music?
What musical instruments have you studied?
What is your favorite song or piece of music?
What is the name of your favorite group?
Who is your favorite singer?
Who is your favorite composer or song writer?
Why do you listen to music?

3. If . . .

In pairs, answer the following question. Then share your answer with the class.

If you could be a famous musician, composer, or singer who would you be? You can choose a living musician (such as Whitney Houston) or a dead one (such as Mozart). Tell why you have chosen that person.

4. Survey

Ask five of the members of your class for the information in the chart below. Compare your list with your classmate's lists. What music is most popular? Which musicians or composers are the most popular

Name	What are your favorite and least favorite kinds of music?	What is your favorite song or musical piece?	Who is your favorite singer or musical group?
1.			
2.			
3.			
4.			
5.			

MUSIC TRANSCRIPT

Amy and Tom have just met at a party.

Amy: Hi, I'm Amy.

Tom: Nice to meet you. I'm Tom. I'm a friend of Carol's from Florida.

Amy: Really!

Tom: Yes, I just got here yesterday.

Amy: How long will you be staying?

Tom: Actually, I'm moving here.

Amy: That's great! Welcome to California!

Tom: Thanks. Ummm . . . what's this music they're playing?

Amy: It's the *Talking Feet*. They're really popular now.

Tom: I've never heard of them.

Amy: It's a new band from Los Angeles.

Tom: Uh-huh.

Amy: They've got a strong rhythm, so they're easy to dance to.

Tom: Their lyrics are really interesting.

Amy: I think so too. The words are very poetic.

Tom: (*pause*) Actually, I don't usually listen to such modern music. I've been listening to a lot of older acoustic music lately.

Amy: Really, what kind of music do you like?

Tom: Spanish guitar and jazz mostly.

Amy: Spanish guitar is so romantic.

Tom: Yeah. (*pause*) I listen to a lot of jazz from the Fifties.

Amy: Do you know Miles Parker?

Tom: Yeah, he's a great saxophone player and composer. I love his Quintet.

Amy: Me too. My father always played his music, so I know it pretty well!

Tom: It's really soothing after a busy day.

Amy: Yeah!

Tom: (*pause*) In Florida, we listen to the blues a lot.

Amy: Isn't Sonny Franklin from Florida?

Tom: Yeah, he's great! His wife is better, though!

Amy: Who's his wife?

Tom: Diamond Tooth Mary Macrae!

Amy: I've never heard of her!

Tom: She's 82 now, but her voice is still really strong.

Amy: (*pause*) Uh . . . do you ever listen to classical music?

Tom: I'm crazy about Mozart and Beethoven, especially when it's played by a large orchestra!

Amy: Me too. What do you think about Bach?

Tom: He's O.K., but I prefer Beethoven to Bach. His music is louder and faster.

Amy: (*pause*) Well, uh, Tom, it's been really nice talking to you. You have to excuse me, but I see my friend just arrived and I need to talk to her.

Tom: No problem. We'll talk later.

Amy: Good idea!

Tom: See you later.

Amy: Yeah.

CHAPTER EIGHT

EXPLANATIONS

LISTENING

Look at the picture. Can you identify any of the objects? What are they? If you can't identify any of the objects, what do you think might be?

Listen to the dialogue and fill in the blanks with T (true) or F (false). Listen again to check your answers.

Brian and Nancy visit Mr. Smith's Curio Shop.

_____ Mr. Smith sells things from Europe only.

_____ A kora is a kind of musical instrument.

_____ Koras come from India.

_____ The raclette machine came from France.

_____ Raclette machines cook cheese and potatoes.

_____ A tansu is a kind of food.

_____ A tansu is used to store clothing.

_____ A tansu usually consists of two parts.

_____ A kotatsu consists of a table and a chair.

_____ Batik is a kind of dyed cloth.

_____ Hammocks are used for sleeping.

_____ Hammocks from the Yucatan Peninsula are made of wool.

_____ Thai Celadon pottery is different from Chinese Celadon pottery.

FROM THE DIALOGUE

Study the vocabulary.

CLASSIFICATION

It **looks like a type of** musical instrument.
It's **a kind of** furniture.

COMPARISON

It's very **similar to** Chinese pottery.
It **looks like** a low table.

NAMING

That's **called** a raclette machine. (called = named)

STRUCTURE

Question
Does it have **two parts?**

Answers
Yes, most tansu **consist of** two
   sections: a top and a bottom.

PURPOSE

Question
What's it **used for?**

Answers
It's **used for** melting a special cheese
   over potatoes.
It's **used to** store clothing.

> Note: *used for* + verb + *ing*
>
>   *used to* + verb

MATERIAL

Question
What's it **made of?**

Answers
They are usually **made from** very
   beautiful   woods.
It's **made of** fine cotton thread.

ORIGIN

Question
Where's it **from?**

Answers
It's **from** the Sahara desert region of Africa.
It **comes from** the Yucatan Peninsula.

CONVERSATION PRACTICE

1. Turn to page 86 and read the dialogue in groups of three. Ask your teacher to explain any vocabulary or grammar you do not understand.

VOCABULARY EXPANSION
Study the additional vocabulary.
COMPARISON
It **sounds like** a police car.   It **tastes like** ice cream.
CONTRAST
Cantonese food **is different from** Hunan food.   Tall **is the opposite** of short.
ORIGIN
The transistor **was (first) developed in** the U.S.A.   Buddhism **was started in** India.
EXAMPLES
Fermentation **is an example of** a chemical process.

2. Complete each sentence with the correct classification.

_____ Shampoo is a kind of . . .   a. tool.

_____ A hammer is a . . .   b. soap.

_____ A sofa is a type of . . .   c. furniture.

tools

3. Complete each sentence with the correct comparison.

_____ An orange is similar to . . .   a. Alabama.

_____ A wolf is similar to . . .   b. a tangerine.

_____ Mississippi is similar to . . .   c. a dog.

_____ Bluegrass music sounds like . . .   d. Japanese cedar trees.

_____ Some snake meat tastes like . . .   e. chicken.

_____ California redwood trees look a lot like . . .   f. Scottish folk music.

4. Complete each sentence with the correct contrast.

_____ European food is different from . . .   a. Asian food.

_____ Cable TV is very different from . . .   b. painting.

_____ Photography is different from . . .   c. black.

_____ White is the opposite of . . .   d. network TV.

5. Complete each sentence with the correct purpose .

_____ A word processor is used to . . .   a. make holes.

_____ Detergent is used for . . .   b. cleaning.

_____ A drill is used to . . .   c. write letters.

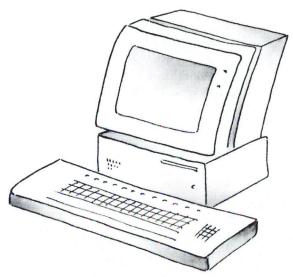

6. Complete each sentence with the correct structure.

_____ A personal computer usually consists of . . .   a. four legs and a top.

_____ The United States consists of . . .   b. 50 states and the District of Columbia.

_____ A table almost always has . . .   c. a keyboard, a CPU, monitor, and a printer.

7. Complete each sentence with the correct material.

_____ Furniture is usually made from . . .   a. ground beef, bread, spices, and an egg.

_____ Meatloaf is made of . . .   b. wood, plastic, or metal.

_____ Knives are usually made from . . .   c. steel.

8. Complete each sentence with the correct origin.

_____ Writing was probably first developed in . . .   a. the U.S.

_____ Jazz started in. . .   b. India.

_____ The game of Chess came from . . .   c. the Middle East.

_____ Noodles were first developed in . . .   d. China.

9. Complete each sentence with the correct example.

_____ French is an example of . . .   a. a Germanic language.

_____ English is an example of . . .   b. a Slavic language.

_____ Russian is an example of . . .   c. a Romance language.

10. Read the explanations and fill in the blanks with the correct words. Use your dictionary when necessary.

1. _____ I am a kind of fruit. I am yellow and long. I grow in bunches. I have a thick peel.

2. _____ I am a kind of animal. I am very large and gray. There are two types of me: Indian and African. I have a long nose (trunk) and large teeth (tusks).

3. _____ I am a kind of wine. I am from northeastern France. I am used at celebrations. I am very bubbly. What am I?

4. _____ I am a kind of tool. I am used to cut wood. I consist of two parts: a handle and a blade.

YOUR TURN

1. It's a Kind of . . .

Write an explanation for each of the following objects. Remember to start with classification (. . . is a kind of . . .). Use your dictionary when necessary. When you finish, compare your answers with your classmates' answers.

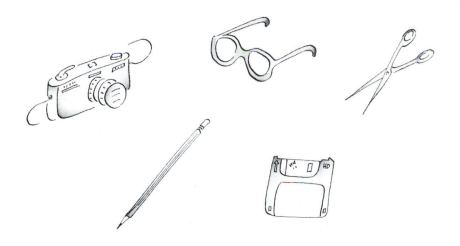

1. a camera: _____

   _____

2. eyeglasses: _____

   _____

3. scissors: _____

   _____

4. a pencil: _____

   _____

5. a floppy disk: _____

   _____

2. Explain It to Me

Variation 1   *The teacher will give you a card with a word on it. Think of an explanation for the word quickly and tell it to the class. (Don't use the word in your explanation!) The class must guess the word. (Teachers: The word cards for this exercise are on page 208 of the Appendix.)*

Variation 2   *Choose a word in English for an object or thing. Think of an explanation for the word and then tell it to the class. (Don't use the word in your explanation!) The class must guess the word.*

Variation 3   *Think of something from your country that the other students will not know (such as a tansu). Think of an explanation. Then tell the class your word and present your explanation.*

EXPLANATIONS TRANSCRIPT

Brian and Nancy visit Mr. Smith's Curio shop.

Brian: Wow, there sure is a lot of stuff here!

Mr. Smith: Yes, I've collected things from almost every country in the world.

Nancy: What's this?

Mr. Smith: It's a kora.

Brian: It looks like a type of musical instrument.

Mr. Smith: It is a musical instrument. The strings are plucked with the thumbs.

Nancy: Where's it from?

Mr. Smith: It's from the Sahara desert region of Africa.

Brian: How about this?

Mr. Smith: That's called a raclette machine. It's from Switzerland.

Brian: What's it used for?

Mr. Smith: It's used for melting a special cheese over potatoes. Pickles and onions are added after it's cooked.

Nancy: How about this?

Mr. Smith: That's from our Japanese section. It's called a tansu.

Nancy: What's it used for?

Mr. Smith: It's a kind of furniture used to store clothing. They are usually made from very beautiful kinds of wood.

Brian: Does it have two parts?

Mr. Smith: Yes, most tansu consist of two sections: a top and a bottom.

Nancy: What's this?

Mr. Smith: That's a kotatsu, also from Japan.

Nancy: Uh-huh. It looks like a low table.

Mr. Smith: Yes, it does, but it consists of a table top, table legs and a heater.

Nancy: A heater?

Mr. Smith: Yes, there's a heater under the table so that people sitting down feel warm.

Nancy: That's amazing!

Brian: Where are all of these cloths from?

Mr. Smith: Those are Indonesian batiks.

Brian: Batiks?

Mr. Smith: Yes, the dying process is very complicated.

Brian: They're beautiful. What are they used for?

Mr. Smith: They are used for anything and everything.

Nancy: This is an incredible shop.

Mr. Smith: I'm glad that you like it.

Brian: What's this?

Mr. Smith: It's a Mexican hammock. It comes from the Yucatan Peninsula.

Brian: A hammock. It's so big.

Mr. Smith: Yes, it's the biggest size. A husband and wife can sleep in it comfortably.

Brian: It's used for sleeping?

Mr. Smith: Yes.

Brian: What's it made of?

Mr. Smith: It's made of fine cotton thread.

Brian: What's this?

Nancy: Is this Chinese pottery?

Mr. Smith: Actually, that's from Thailand. It's called Celadon.

Nancy: It's very similar to Chinese pottery.

Mr. Smith: Yes, you're right. The Celadon technique came from China. (*pause*) Well, I need to be getting back to work.

Nancy: Thank you very much for showing us your shop. Can we keep looking around?

Mr. Smith: Yes, feel free to stay as long as you want. I'll be in the office if you need me.

Brian: Thanks.

Mr. Smith: Come in later and we'll have some tea.

Nancy: We'll do that.

CHAPTER NINE

FOOD

LISTENING

Look at the picture. Every country has it's own food specialties. What are some of the specialties in your country? How are they made?

Listen to the dialogue and fill in the blanks with T (true) or F (false). Listen again to check your answers.

Kim and Harry are trying to decide where to go for a meal.

_____ Kim is very hungry.

_____ Kim wants to get takeout food and then eat at home.

_____ Harry wants to eat Chinese food.

_____ Kim thinks that Japanese food is too spicy.

_____ Kim loves horseradish.

_____ Kim wants to eat Mexican food.

_____ Harry does not want to eat spicy food.

_____ Kim is trying to lose weight.

_____ Kim wants to eat French food because it has few calories.

_____ Kim suggests a vegetarian restaurant, the Harvest Home Cafe.

_____ Harry loves soyburgers and grains.

_____ Harry suggests Burger City.

_____ Harry offers to pay for the meal.

FROM THE DIALOGUE

Study the vocabulary.

TALKING ABOUT FOOD

<u>Questions</u>

Do you want to go to a restaurant **or would you rather** get takeout?

What kind of food do you want to eat?

<u>Suggestions</u>

Why don't we go get something to eat?

How about Chinese**?**

What about Japanese**?**

Let's eat Mexican food.

Afterwards, we could go somewhere for a cup of coffee.

IDIOMS: DECIDING WHAT TO EAT

I'm **starving to death.** = I'm very hungry.

I **don't feel like having** anything too spicy. = I don't want anything too spicy.

Thai cooking **is out.** = I don't want Thai food.

I'm afraid so.

I'm **on a diet.** = I want to lose weight.

I could really **use a** salad right now. = I would really like a salad.

All of that fat in beef is really **bad for** your heart. = unhealthy

They're **good for you.**

I'll **pass on** the cake. = I don't want any cake.

I'll buy.

So it's settled.

I guess so. / I guess that would be O.K.

We'll see.

SPECIAL FOOD WORDS

calorie = a measure of the amount of heat or energy in food

cuisine = a national style of cooking

grains (for example: wheat and rye)

salad bar = a counter where a customer can choose from many vegetables and dressings

soyburger = artificial hamburger made from soy beans

spices (for example: cinnamon, cloves, and nutmeg)

takeout = food prepared by a restaurant to be eaten elsewhere

vegetarian = no meat

Yuck! = an expression of distaste

ADJECTIVES FOR FOOD

beautiful	**healthy**	**so-so**
bland	**low-fat**	**sour**
boring	**nutritious**	**spicy**
delicious	**rich**	**subtle (delicate)**
disgusting	**salty**	**sweet**
greasy (oily)		

CONVERSATION PRACTICE

1. Turn to page 94 and read the dialogue in pairs. Ask your teacher explain any vocabulary or grammar you do not understand.

Spicy!

2. Match the word or expression in Column One with the similar word or expression in Column Two.

Column One

_____ bland

_____ spicy

_____ Yuck!

_____ nutritious

_____ It's just so-so.

_____ I'm starving to death.

_____ Why don't we get a salad?

_____ I don't feel like having a salad.

_____ I'm on a diet.

_____ I guess that would be O.K.

_____ It's settled.

_____ vegetarian

_____ I'll pass on the cake.

_____ I'll buy.

_____ We'll see.

Column Two

a. It's good for you.

b. no meat

c. mild

d. We've made a decision.

e. It's just OK.

f. I'm really hungry.

g. I will pay.

h. I don't really want to, but I'll do it.

i. We will decide later.

j. I'm trying to lose weight.

k. I don't really want a salad.

l. That's disgusting!

o. hot

n. How about a salad?

p. no cake for me

3. In pairs, give one example of a food for each of the adjectives. The first one is done for you. When you finish, compare your answers with your classmates' answers.

1. sweet   _chocolate cake_

2. bland   _____

3. spicy   _____

4. greasy   _____

5. beautiful   _____

6. delicious   _____

7. salty   _____

8. rich   _____

9. nutritious   _____

10. disgusting   _____

11. boring   _____

12. subtle   _____

13. so-so   _____

14. low-fat   _____

15. sour   _____

YOUR TURN

1. What Do You Eat?

*In pairs, answer the two questions. The listener should respond to the speaker, using listener expressions (**Uh-huh, That sounds delicious!**) and ask more questions.*

1. Describe the food in your country. Is it sweet, sour, spicy, etc.?
   What meats, vegetables, etc. are eaten?
2. Describe a typical meal in your home. What is eaten for breakfast, lunch, and dinner?

2. Food Groups

In pairs, study the picture. Discuss how much of each food group you eat in one day. Then make suggestions to your partner of how he/she could improve his/her diet. For example:
You should eat more rice.

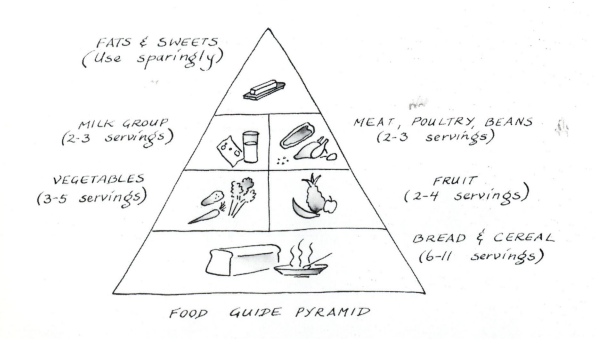

2. Survey

Ask five members of your class for the information in the chart below. Give complete answers. When you finish, discuss your findings with your classmates.

Name	What is your favorite food? Why?	What is the strangest food you have ever eaten?	What country's food do you like the best? Why?	What is your favorite restaurant? Why?
1.				
2.				
3.				
4.				
5.				

FOOD TRANSCRIPT

Kim and Harry are trying to decide where to go for a meal.

Kim: I'm starving to death. Why don't we go get something to eat.

Harry: Do you want to go to a restaurant or would you rather get takeout?

Kim: Let's go to a restaurant.

Harry: What kind of food do you want to eat?

Kim: How about Chinese? I know a place where they make great sweet and sour pork.

Harry: Well, I don't really like Chinese food, especially pork.

Kim: Why not?

Harry: I don't know. The taste is just so-so. What about Japanese? Their food is so beautiful.

Kim: Japanese food is so bland— it's boring! Besides, it's too salty.

Harry: Japanese food isn't bland, it's subtle.

Kim: Sure it's bland. There are no spices. It all tastes the same.

Harry: It's true that there are few spices, but they use wasabi, ginger, shiso and . . .

Kim: What's wasabi?

Harry: It's a plant that's similar to horseradish.

Kim: I hate horseradish!

Harry: Well, then, let me see . . .

Kim: Let's eat Mexican food! It's my favorite!

Harry: Not today. I don't feel like having anything too spicy.

Kim: Well, if you don't want spicy food, Thai cooking is out.

Harry: I'm afraid so. (*pause*) Hey, isn't there a new French restaurant near your house?

Kim: We can't eat French. It's too rich and I'm on a diet.

Harry: But the new French cuisine doesn't have as much fat.

Kim: It's still too many calories.

Harry: You're probably right. I should lose a few pounds myself.

Kim: I know. Let's go to the vegetarian restaurant on Third Street.

Harry: Which one?

Kim: The Harvest Home Cafe.

Harry: I don't know it. I've never gone there.

Kim: It's great! They have a huge salad bar and soyburgers.

Harry: Soyburgers?

Kim: They're delicious and nutritious! They also have vegetable dishes with different kinds of grains.

Harry: Grains? You mean like wheat and rye?

Kim: Sure! They're good for you!

Harry: No, I don't think so, but how about Burger City.

Kim: Yuck! Burgers are too greasy! They're disgusting and all of that fat in beef is really bad for your heart.

Harry: But Burger City also has a fantastic salad bar and I can get a hamburger and some French fries.

Kim: Well, I guess that would be O.K. I could really use a salad right now.

Harry: And they have low-fat chocolate cake!

Kim: The salad sounds good, but I'll pass on the cake.

Harry: I'll buy.

Kim: That sounds even better.

Harry: So it's settled.

Kim: I guess so.

Harry: And afterwards we could go somewhere for some nice jazz and a cup of coffee.

Kim: We'll see.

Harry: O.K., let's go!

CHAPTER TEN

REDUCED FORMS

LISTENING

Listen to the dialogue and fill in the blanks with T (true) or F (false). Listen again to check your answers.

Two teenagers, Pam and Stan, are discussing their futures.

_____ Stan has been waiting a long time.

_____ Stan is thinking about his life after high school.

_____ Stan does not know what to do after high school.

_____ Pam wants to be an airline stewardess.

_____ Stan knows a great deal about geography.

_____ Stan likes high school.

_____ Pam has to go see her aunt.

_____ Pam and Stan will meet the next day at 8:00 to go to the movies.

FROM THE DIALOGUE

*When people are speaking quickly some sounds change or disappear. Study the reduced forms (in **bold type**). Learn to recognize reduced forms, but be careful using them. These forms are normally spoken, but NOT WRITTEN!*

STANDARD ENGLISH	TRANSFORMATION	REDUCED LANGUAGE
(Have) you been here long?	you ➟ **ya** here ➟ **'ere**	**Ya** been **'ere** long?
What are you doing?	what are you ➟ **wha-der-ya** -ing ➟ **-in'**	**Wha-der-ya** doin'?
I'm just thinking about what I ought to do after high school.	about ➟ **'bout** ought to ➟ **awda**	I'm just **thinkin' 'bout wha-die-awda** do after high school.
What do you want to do after you graduate?	what do you ➟ **wha-dya** (what did you ➟ **wha-dja**) want to ➟ **wanna** **Note:** _do you_ alone may reduce to _dya_.	**Wha-dya wanna** do after **ya** graduate?
I don't know.	don't know ➟ **dunno**	I **dunno**.
I'm going to be a pilot because they get to go wherever they want to.	going to ➟ **gonna** because ➟ **'cause** get to ➟ **getta**	I'm **gonna** be a pilot. **'cause** they **getta** go wherever they **wanna**.
I want to go to Indonesia and France.	to ➟ **da** and ➟ **'n'**	I **wanna** go **da** Indonesia **'n'** France.
Don't you know anything about geography?	don't you ➟ **don-chya**	**Don-chya** know anything **'bout** geography?
You have to study harder.	have to ➟ **hafta** (has to ➟ **hasta**)	**Ya hafta** study harder.
I want to get out of here.	out of ➟ **ouda**	I **wanna** get **ouda** here.

IDIOMS

have a blast = have fun
lousy = bad / poor quality

CONVERSATION PRACTICE

*1. Turn to page 101 and read the dialogue in pairs. Ask your teacher to explain any vocabulary or grammar you do not understand. Try to pronounce the **BOLD** words as reduced forms. If necessary, listen to the tape again.*

VOCABULARY EXPANSION

STANDARD ENGLISH	TRANSFORMATION	REDUCED LANGUAGE
What did he want?	what did he ➡ **wha-dee**	**Wha-dee** want?
Do you know the time?	do you ➡ **dya**	**Dya** know the time?
Won't you please come?	won't you? ➡ **won-chya?**	**Won-chya** please come?
Is this your hat?	your ➡ **yer**	Is this **yer** hat?
She must have been sick.	must have ➡ **must-uv**	She **must-uv** been sick.

<u>DICTATION</u>

Listen to the 20 sentences. Write them down in standard English, not reduced forms. When you finish, compare your sentences with your classmates' sentences and read them aloud as reduced forms. (Teachers: The tapescript for this exercise is on page 210 of the Appendix.)

1. _____
2. _____
3. _____
4. _____
5. _____
6. _____
7. _____
8. _____
9. _____
10. _____
11. _____
12. _____
13. _____
14. _____
15. _____
16. _____
17. _____
18. _____
19. _____
20. _____

2. **Read the following sentences and circle any words or phrases which can be said in reduced form. When you finish, practice reading the sentences in pairs.**

   1. What do you know about South America?

   2. Do you like sushi?

   3. What are you thinking about?

   4. I don't know.

   5. I want to go hiking.

   6. You have to do it!

   7. He ought to be working.

   8. Do you not like rock and roll?

   9. How are you going to do it?

   10. What did he say?

Wha-dya know about South America?

YOUR TURN

Survey

Ask five members of your class for the information in the chart below. Be sure to pronounce all your questions and answers in reduced form. When you finish, compare your answers with your classmates' answers.

Name	What are you going to do next weekend?	What do you want to do with your life?	What do you want to do after you finish school?
1.			
2.			
3.			
4.			
5.			

REDUCED FORMS TRANSCRIPT

Two teenagers, Pam and Stan, are discussing their futures.

Pam: Hi Stan. **You** been **here** long?

Stan: No, I just got **here**.

Pam: **What are you doing**?

Stan: **Nothing** much. I'm just **thinking about** what I **ought to** do after high school.

Pam: **What do you want to** do after **you** graduate?

Stan: I **don't know. What do you want to** do?

Pam: I'm **going to** be a pilot **because** they **get to** go wherever they **want to**.

Stan: Where do **you want to** go?

Pam: I **want to** go to Indonesia **and** France.

Stan: Indonesia?

Pam: It's in Asia. **Don't you** know anything **about** geography?

Stan: Nah, I had a lousy teacher for geography.

Pam: **You have to** study harder, Stan, or you'll stay in high school forever.

Stan: That's O.K. with me. High school is really interesting. I'm **having** a blast!

Pam: I really like it too, but someday I **want to** get **out of** here.

Stan: Hey, why don't we go out for lunch?

Pam: I can't. I'm **going to** go see my uncle.

Stan: That's too bad! Maybe we can have lunch some other time.

Pam: Yeah, but I'll see **you** tomorrow anyway. We're **going to** go **to** the movies, right?

Stan: Yeah, I'll see **you** at 8:00.

Pam: Bye.

REVIEW

CHAPTERS 1-10

1. Conversation Analysis

In pairs, read the two conversations and decide which one is better and which one is worse.

Conversation 1: At a cocktail party, Gabriella approaches Aki.

Gabriella:	Hello.
Aki:	Hello.
Gabriella:	How are you?
Aki:	Fine, thank you.
Gabriella:	Where are you from?
Aki:	Japan.
Gabriella:	Do you like the US?
Aki:	Yes.
Gabriella:	How long have you been here?
Aki:	(*silence*)
Gabriella:	When did you come to the US?
Aki:	Two years ago.
Gabriella:	Good-bye.
Aki:	Good-bye.

Conversation 2: At a cocktail party, Norihiko and Gabriella talk.

Gabriella:	Hello.
Norihiko:	Hello, I'm Norihiko.
Gabriella:	I'm Gabriella. Where are you from?
Norihiko:	I'm from Japan.
Gabriella:	What city?
Norihiko:	I'm from a city called Odawara. You probably haven't heard of it.
Gabriella:	No, I haven't. What's it like?
Norihiko:	It's actually quite beautiful!
Gabriella:	Really?
Norihiko:	Yes, it's on Sagami Bay and it's at the edge of Hakone, a mountainous region full of hot springs.
Gabriella:	So it has mountains and the sea?
Norihiko:	Yes, that's right!
Gabriella:	It sounds fantastic!!
Norihiko:	Yes, it is beautiful. (*pause*) Where are you from?
Gabriella:	I'm originally from Peru, but I've lived here for twenty years, so it's my home now.
Norihiko:	I've been here only two years.
Gabriella:	How do you like it here?
Norihiko:	Well, I like the personal freedom that Americans have, but sometimes I don't like living in the city.
Gabriella:	Because of the social problems?
Norihiko:	Yes, I worry about my wife coming home alone sometimes.
Gabriella:	I know what you mean. My husband works downtown and I'm always worried that someone will try to rob him or something.
Norihiko:	The museums are wonderful here, though.
Gabriella:	Yes, they certainly are. (*pause*)
Norihiko:	Well, it was nice talking to you. I need to get another drink , and there are a lot of people I haven't talked to yet.
Gabriella:	And I should really talk a little more to our host.
Norihiko:	I should too.
Gabriella:	We can talk a little more later.
Norihiko:	Good idea!
Gabriella:	See you later!
Norihiko:	Bye.

Which conversation is better? Which is worse? List all the positive points of the better conversation and all the negative points of the worse conversation. When you finish, discuss your opinions with the class.

2. Listener Cues

Complete the conversation with appropriate expressions. The first one is done for you.

A: Sylvia, it's so nice to see you again!

B: Bob, how have you been?

A: Not so well. I was sick all last week.

B: *Oh, that's too bad!* _____

A: And my wife lost her job.

B: _____

A: Then, my 16-year-old son announced that he's getting married.

B: _____

A: How have *you* been?

B: I've been doing quite well. I've finally found a publisher for my book.

A: _____

B: And my daughter just gave birth to a baby boy.

A: _____

B: Unfortunately, it's not all good news. My mother died last month.

A: _____

B: She had a really good long life, though. She was 97 years old!

A: _____

B: Well, I've got to go. I certainly hope that things will get better for you.

A: I do too. Say hello to Bob.

B: I will. Bye.

A: Bye!

3. Matching

Match the sentences in Column One with the sentences in Column Two. The first one is done for you.

Column One	Column Two
_b_ Did you have a nice weekend?	a. Poland
____ What's up?	b. No, I just stayed home.
____ I'd like you to meet my wife.	c. It's very beautiful.
____ My dog died.	d. I went skiing.
____ Where are you from?	e. It's nice to meet you.
____ Well, I'd better be going.	f. I like it very much!
____ We'll have to get together sometime.	g. I guess it is getting late.
____ How do you like New York?	h. I'm so sorry to hear that.
____ What's New Hampshire like?	i. That would be nice.
____ What did you do?	j. Nothing much.

4. Open Questions

Put an X in front of any open question.

____ How old are you?

____ Why did you choose Spain?

____ What's it like?

____ What's your name?

____ How'd you like it?

____ What do you think about it?

How do you like New York?

Write three more open questions.

1. _____

2. _____

3. _____

5. Vocabulary

Fill in the blanks with words from the list.

Florida is really hot and humid in the summer.

humid	foggy	like	freezing	weather

1. Florida is really hot and _____ in the summer.

2. It's _____ cold! I'll have to put on a sweater.

3. Where's the sun? I hate it when it's _____ like this!

4. What's the weather _____ in your country?

5. I love the _____ in Alaska. It's so nice in the summer.

lyrics	acoustic	soothing	bluegrass	traditional

1. Folk music is very _____. It always relaxes me.

2. I don't like modern music. I prefer _____ music.

3. After living in Kentucky for ten years, I started to love _____ music.

4. Electric guitars are too loud, so I studied _____ guitar.

5. I never listen to the _____ of songs, only the music.

kind of	used for	similar to	made from	came from

1. Bread is _____ flour, water and yeast.

2. A saw is a _____ tool.

3. The game of chess _____ India.

4. Tangerines are _____ oranges.

5. Computers are _____ writing letters and storing information.

bland	spicy	on a diet	bad for you	why don't we

1. Too much fat in food is _____.

2. I can't eat chocolate because I'm _____.

3. Mexican food is too _____ for me.

4. _____ go out to eat tonight?

5. Food in the United States is too _____ for me. I like hot food.

6. Reduced Forms

Listen to the ten sentences. Write them down in standard English. (Teachers: The tapescript for this exercise is on page 211 of the Appendix.)

1. _____
2. _____
3. _____
4. _____
5. _____
6. _____
7. _____
8. _____
9. _____
10. _____

7. Scrambled Conversation

Put the conversation in the correct order by numbering the sentences. The first one is done for you. Ask your teacher to explain any expressions you do not understand. When you finish, compare your answers with a classmate's answers.

_____ I'm doing fine. Hey, you look great! Did you lose some weight?

_____ Not bad, Andy. How about yourself?

_____ Hmmmm, well, yeah. I'd love to come.

_____ 6:00? I'll be there!

_____ Yeah, I've been getting more exercise and eating less.

_____ I'll see you then.

___1___ Hey, Jack! How're you doing?

_____ Great! Be at my house at 6:00 Saturday morning.

_____ That's wonderful. I should do that too. Hey, that reminds me. I'm going to go fishing with my family this weekend. You want to come?

_____ So long!

CHAPTER ELEVEN

SCHOOL

LISTENING

Listen to each dialogue and fill in the blanks with T (true) or F (false). Listen again to check your answers.

1. Susie and Bess are discussing the final examinations at their high school.

_____ Jeff, Susie's boyfriend, will probably fail the examinations.

_____ Jeff studies hard every night.

_____ Jeff will take tests in chemistry and English tomorrow.

_____ Jeff has average grades right now.

_____ Susie likes Jeff because he is cute.

2. Jeff and Susie are talking after the test.

_____ Jeff did well on the biology test.

_____ He studied hard for it the night before.

_____ Jeff thinks that he also did well on the English test.

_____ Jeff is now a junior.

_____ Susie's parents don't like Jeff.

3. John and Mike, two college freshmen, meet.

_____ John has a history test tomorrow.

_____ Mike tells John to study the next morning.

_____ Mike is worried about his grades.

_____ John is majoring in education.

_____ Mike thinks that education is an easy major.

FROM THE DIALOGUES

Study the vocabulary.

GRADES
---

grades = a rating system (A = excellent, B = good, C = average, D = poor, F = fail)
has a D = his grade is D
got an F / flunk / bomb = to fail, to receive a grade of F
Ace = to do well, to receive a high grade (A)

PROBLEMS IN SCHOOL
---

drop out = to stop going to school

goof off = to be lazy, to have fun rather than study

cutting class / skipping class = not going to class

give (someone) **a hard time** = to cause a problem for someone, to make life difficult for someone

---
TALKING ABOUT SUCCESS OR FAILURE
---

sounds pretty hopeless = there is little chance of success
No way! = It's impossible!
a breeze = easy
No problem! = Don't worry! Everything is OK!

TALKING ABOUT STUDIES
---

pull an all nighter = to study all night
cram = to study very hard for a short period of time before a test
a killer course = a difficult class
tests = examinations
a really big test = an important test
attendance = the number of times present in class
bookworm = someone who always studies

HIGHER EDUCATION
---

major = the main subject a person studies (an English major)
degree = a certificate that you receive when you finish a program of study
grad school = studies for a very advanced degree in a university;
  for example: Master of Arts, Ph.D.
BA = Bachelor of Arts Degree = a basic degree usually received after four or five years of work
MA = Masters of Arts Degree = for two/three years work after a bachelor's degree
Ph.D. = the highest degree; it may take 7 years after the bachelor's degree
freshman, sophomore, junior, senior = years of high school / university (first, second, third, and fourth years)

CONVERSATION PRACTICE

1. *Turn to page 118 and read the dialogues in pairs. Ask your teacher to explain any vocabulary or grammar you do not understand.*

2. *Match the sentences in Column One with the sentences in Column Two. The first one is done for you.*

An all-nighter

Column One

__l__ She says that she can pull an all nighter.

_____ He's just been goofing off!

_____ He's always cutting class.

_____ He's always giving the teacher a hard time.

_____ No way!

_____ It was a breeze!

_____ I crammed for it.

_____ I'm sure that I aced the test!

_____ No problem!

_____ I bombed that one.

_____ English is a killer course for me.

_____ I'm really scared he's going to flunk.

_____ You're such a bookworm.

_____ What's your major?

_____ I'll probably drop out for a while.

Column Two

a. What's that main subject that you are studying?

b. I studied intensively for a short time.

c. I'll probably stop going to school for a while.

d. Don't worry about it!

e. He doesn't cooperate with his teacher.

f. It is a very difficult class for me.

g. I'm afraid that he will fail his tests.

h. He hasn't been working hard.

i. I did badly.

j. It's impossible.

k. You are always studying!

l. She can study all night.

m. It was easy.

n. He is often absent from class.

o. I'm sure that I did very well on the exam.

YOUR TURN

1. "In My Country . . . "

Prepare a short description of education in your country. Answer some or all of the questions below. Then present this information to the class.

> How many years do you study?
>
> What are universities like?
>
> What are the main subjects?
>
> What is the relationship like between students and teachers?
>
> How many hours/day, days/week, weeks/year do students go to class?
>
> What are the major rules for students to follow?
>
> How is education in your country different from education in other countries? How is it similar?

2. If . . .

In pairs, answer the following question. Then share your answers with the class.

If you could go to any school in the world and study anything that you wanted to (all expenses paid), where would you go and what would you study?

They give him a hard time.

3. Survey

Ask five members of your class for the information in the chart below. When you finish, compare your answers with your classmate's answers.

Name	What is your favorite subject?	What is the most boring subject?	What do you want to do after graduation?
1.			
2.			
3.			
4.			
5.			

SCHOOL TRANSCRIPT

1. Susie and Bess are discussing the final examinations at their high school.

Susie: I'm really scared that my boyfriend Jeff's going to flunk his exams.

Bess: Why, Susie?

Susie: He's just been goofing off. He says that he can pull an all nighter tonight and do O.K.

Bess: How many tests does he have tomorrow?

Susie: Two—biology and English.

Bess: What're his grades now?

Susie: Bad. He's flunking biology and he has a D in English.

Bess: That's bad all right!

Susie: He's always cutting class to ride his motorcycle or giving the teacher a hard time.

Bess: That's terrible! Uh . . . why do you like him?

Susie: He's real cute and he's really nice to me.

Bess: What do your parents think?

Susie: They say that if he fails this year, I'll have to find another boyfriend.

Bess: Maybe he'll pass.

Susie: No way!

2: Jeff and Susie are talking after the test.

Susie: How'd you do?

Jeff: No problem! Biology was a breeze. I crammed all night for it and Mr. Johnson asked everything I knew.

Susie: Really?

Jeff: I'm sure that I aced it!

Susie: How about English?

Jeff: I bombed that one. English has always been a killer course for me. It's like a foreign language!

Susie: You think you got an F?

Jeff: It all depends on whether or not Ms. Jackson wants to give me a hard time.

Susie: Oh yeah?

Jeff: My attendance hasn't been too bad in her class and I only fell asleep a couple of times.

Susie: It sounds pretty hopeless to me!

Jeff: Only in English! And I could pull out a D- in English.

Susie: If you don't pass this year, you'll be a junior again.

Jeff: Your Dad'd love that.

3. John and Mike, two college freshmen, meet.

Mike: Hey John! Let's go out and have some fun!

John: I can't Mike. I have to take a really big history test tomorrow.

Mike: So wake up early and cram for it tomorrow morning.

John: Actually, I'd rather not.

Mike: Man, you're such a bookworm! When are you going to learn how to relax?

John: After graduation.

Mike: Graduation? You're a freshman!

John: I want to make sure I have good grades for my BA. Then, I'll be able to go to grad school and get an MA or even a Ph.D.

Mike: You could always drop out for a semester or two to have some fun!

John: Forget it! (*pause*) Mike, it's been nice talking to you, but I really have to go.

Mike: Hey, what's your major?

John: Education. Mike, I'll see you tomorrow in class.

Mike: John, what're you so worried about? Everybody knows that no one in education ever flunks!

John: Mike, I've got to go.

Mike: Well, O.K. See you around.

John: Bye.

CHAPTER TWELVE

NON–WORDS

LISTENING

How many words for yes and no do you have in your native language? Be sure to include informal words.

Listen to each dialogue and fill in the blanks with T (true) or F (false). Listen again to check your answers.

1. A couple is sitting in their car in their driveway. They are starting a long trip.

_____ The husband forgot to turn off the gas.

_____ The husband remembered his credit cards.

_____ The wife paid the newspaper girl.

_____ The husband forgot his glasses.

_____ They remembered the maps.

_____ The wife dropped the maps.

_____ The wife gave John the telephone number of the hotel.

2. *Mel and Ken are talking about a rock concert.*

_____ Ken went to The Demented Ratboys concert.

_____ The Demented Ratboys will play another concert that night.

_____ The Demented Ratboys had a backup band.

_____ The Bongo Twins played a long time.

_____ Ken has trouble getting in touch with Mel sometimes.

_____ Ken doesn't have much money.

3. *A mother is worried about her child, Sarah.*

_____ Sarah has a slight fever.

_____ Sarah wants to go to school.

_____ Sarah plays the clarinet.

FROM THE DIALOGUES

Study the vocabulary.

NON-WORDS

Uh-huh ↗ (rising intonation) = Yes
Uh-uh ↘ (falling intonation) = No
Huh? ↗ (not a polite form) = I don't understand.
Uh-oh! ↘ = There is a problem.
Yeah = Yes
Nah = No
Oops! = I dropped something / made a mistake.
Ouch! = I hurt myself.
Yuck! = I don't like something.
Wow! = Great! / Wonderful!

O.K.

O.K. has three meanings.
<u>Yes</u>
A: Would you call my mom next time?
B: **O.K.**

<u>How is your health?</u>
A: Are you **O.K.?**
B: No, I don't feel good.

<u>Asking for permission</u>
A: Mom, is it **O.K.** if I go to school today?
B: No, I think it would be better for you to stay home and rest.

SLANG / IDIOMS

What've you been up to? = What have you been doing lately?
I'm kind of short this week. = I don't have much money this week.
What a drag! = That's too bad.
an opening band = a band that plays before a famous band

FILLERS

Fillers are expressions in conversations which have no meaning. Young people and nervous people tend to use them to fill silences while they are thinking. Learn to recognize them, but don't use them! They make you sound uneducated or unsophisticated.
you know
uh
like

Example: I wish, **like**, you'd have, **you know**, told me.

CONVERSATION PRACTICE

1. Turn to page 126 and read the read the dialogues in pairs. Ask your teacher to explain any vocabulary or grammar you do not understand.

*2. In pairs, take turns asking each other the following questions. Answer with **Uh-huh**, **Uh-uh**, **Yeah**, or **Nah**. Circle whether your partner's response was Yes or No.*

1. Did you watch TV last night?	Yes	No
2. Do you like driving in the mountains?	Yes	No
3. Do you like classical music?	Yes	No
4. Can you give me some money?	Yes	No
5. Is it O.K. if I go home now?	Yes	No
6. Did you have a nice weekend?	Yes	No
7. Are you O.K.?	Yes	No
8. Did you eat breakfast this morning?	Yes	No
9. Is it O.K. if I give you $10?	Yes	No
10. Have you ever been to New York?	Yes	No

3. *Match the sentences in Column One with the responses in Column Two. The first one is done for you.*

Ouch!

Oops!

Column One

_g_ Huh?

_____ Hey Ma! Is it O.K. if I go to Tommy's house?

_____ Oops!

_____ Ouch!

_____ Yuck!

_____ Are you O.K.?

_____ Uh-oh

_____ Is it O.K. if I eat this piece of cake?

Column Two

a. What's the matter?

b. O.K., but don't stay out too late!

c. Doesn't it taste good?

d. No, it's not! It's for your Aunt Thelma!

e. Did you drop something?

f. Did you hurt yourself?

g. Do you want me to say it again?

h. Yeah. I'm fine.

YOUR TURN

Plan a Trip

You are going on a trip across the United States from Los Angeles to New York City. You have four weeks to travel. In pairs, plan the trip. What places in the U.S. would you like to visit? How long would you like to stay in each place? Use the map below or another map.

In your discussion, use these phrases.

Is it O.K. if we visit . . . ?
Would it be O.K. if we visited . . . ?
Do you want to see . . . ?
Can we drive to . . . ?
I'd really like to go to . . .

Give a short presentation to the class about your plan. You should tell the class where you are going, how long you will stay in each place, and why you chose those places.

✓ *(Teachers: For this activity, it may be useful to provide students with a large map of the United States and a guidebook.)*

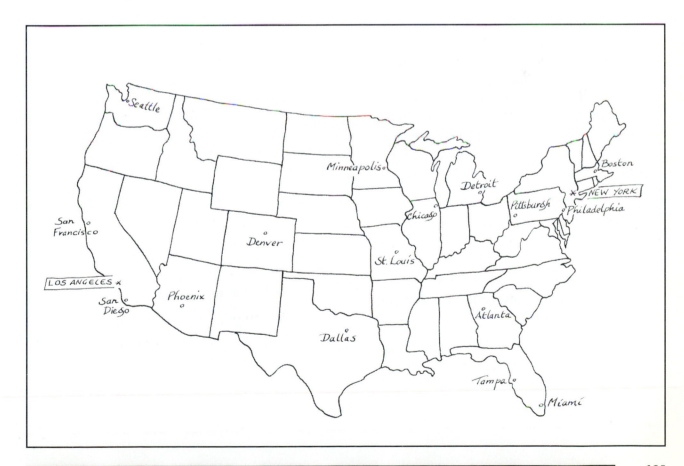

NON-WORDS TRANSCRIPT

1. A couple is sitting in their car in their driveway. They are starting a long trip.

Wife: Did you turn off the gas?

Husband: Huh?

Wife: I said, "Did you turn off the gas?"

Husband: Uh-huh. I turned it off just a minute ago.

Wife: Good! Did you remember your credit cards?

Husband: Uh-huh. Did you pay the newspaper girl?

Wife: Uh-huh. You didn't forget your glasses, did you?

Husband: Uh-uh. Did we remember the maps?

Wife: Uh-huh, I've got them right here in my lap. (*pause*) Oops!

Husband: What happened?

Wife: I dropped my cup of coffee on my shoe.

Husband: Yuck!! Here, I'll help you clean it up.

Wife: Ouch!

Husband: Are you O.K.?

Wife: No, I'm not. I hit my head on the dashboard when I bent down to get my cup.

Husband: You should be more careful.

Wife: Thanks for the advice! (*pause*)

Husband: Did you give John the phone number of the hotel?

Wife: Uh-uh. I didn't have the chance. I'll call him from Nevada.

Husband: Is there anything else?

Wife: Uh-uh. We've got everything.

Husband: O.K., let's go. (*pause*) Uh-oh!

Wife: What's wrong?

Husband: Where are the car keys?

Wife: I don't know. I thought that you had them.

2. Mel and Ken are talking about a rock concert.

Mel: Hey Ken, what've you been up to?

Ken: Nothing much, Mel. Oh! I, uh, went to a great concert last night!

Mel: Oh yeah? Who was it?

Ken: The Demented Ratboys.

Mel: Wow! I didn't even know, you know, that they were in town! Uh, are they playing tonight?

Ken: Nah, they're, like, uh, already on the way to Chicago.

Mel: Was there, uh, an opening band?

Ken: Yeah, the Bongo Twins opened the show.

Mel: Really? Did they, like, uh, play long?

Ken: Nah, only five songs.

Mel: I wish, like, you'd have, you know, told me.

Ken: Well, you know, it's like, uh, kind of difficult to get in touch with you sometimes, man!

Mel: Yeah, but, uh, would you call my mom next time?

Ken: O.K., next time they're in town we'll go together.

Mel: O.K. Hey, man. Have you got a few bucks I can, uh, borrow.

Ken: Sorry man. I'm kind of short this week. I spent it all on the concert.

Mel: What a drag!

3. A mother is worried about her child, Sarah.

Mother: Sarah honey, are you O.K.?

Sarah: No, I don't feel good.

Mother: Your forehead's a little hot!

Sarah: Is it O.K. if I go to school today? I have to practice clarinet with the band.

Mother: No, I think it would be better for you to stay home and rest. If you're O.K. tomorrow, you can go to school then. Is that O.K. with you?

Sarah: I guess so.

CHAPTER THIRTEEN

PEOPLE

LISTENING

Look at the picture. What words would you use to describe the different people?

Listen to the dialogue and fill in the blanks with T (true) or F (false). Listen again to check your answers.

Helen and Mary, two high school seniors, are talking about their classmates.

_____ Mary is dating Bob.

_____ Mary thinks that Bob is cute.

_____ Bill is intelligent.

_____ Helen likes Bill.

_____ Helen is dating Bill.

_____ Rick likes sports.

_____ Rick and Bill play tennis every Saturday.

_____ Both of the young women like Peter.

_____ Betty was dating Peter.

_____ Keith is a high school student.

_____ Keith is intelligent, but has problems with people.

_____ Mary and Helen both like Matt.

_____ Matt has a motorcycle.

FROM THE DIALOGUE

Study the vocabulary. Some of these words are very impolite. Learn to recognize them, but be very careful using them. Asterisks (*) mark dangerous words.

IDIOMS FOR DATING

ask out = to ask someone to go out on a date (to go to a movie; to go out to dinner)
going out (with) = to date; to do things together
going steady (with) = to go out on dates with only one person
broke up with / dumped = ended the relationship

WORDS FOR PEOPLE

a brain = someone who is very intelligent
a creep* = a very bad person
cute = physically attractive
a good conversationalist = someone who is interesting to talk to; a good listener
a jock = an athlete
macho = overly-masculine
mature = adult-like
a nice guy = a good/kind person
a nerd* = someone who lacks social skills
a redneck* = an unsophisticated or uneducated person often from a rural area
rude = impolite
a slob = a person who dresses poorly; someone who is messy
a snob = someone who thinks that he/she is better than other people
a sweetheart = a very nice person   **NOTE:** This word is used primarily by women.
has zero social skills = is awkward in social situations
vegetarian = someone who does not eat meat

CONVERSATION PRACTICE

1. Turn to page 133 and read the dialogue in pairs. Ask your teacher to explain any vocabulary or grammar you do not understand.

Harry   Matthew

2. Read about each person and fill in the blank with the word or words that describe that person. In some cases, more than one word may be appropriate. The first one is done for you.

___nerd___ 1. Harry never wears fashionable clothes. He is very shy. He studies hard. He feels awkward in social situations.

_____ 2. Joe lives on a farm. He's very conservative and feels uncomfortable in town.

_____ 3. Paul treats his girlfriend badly.

_____ 4. Diane is extremely intelligent and studies all the time.

_____ 5. Anne is a really nice person.

_____ 6. Women usually think that Tony is handsome.

_____ 7. Matthew is very strong and loves sports.

_____ 8. People always enjoy talking to Pam.

_____ 9. Harry never does anything selfish or childish.

_____ 10. Jean wears dirty clothes that are too big for her. She rarely cleans her apartment.

YOUR TURN

1. Describe Someone

In pairs, describe someone you know using the words in the list and give details. When you finish, tell the class one or two of your examples.

Example: My brother is a slob. His room is always messy and his clothes are always dirty.

a brain	a nerd
a creep	a redneck
cute	rude
a good conversationalist	a slob
a jock	a snob
macho	a sweetheart
mature	has zero social skills
a nice guy	a vegetarian

2. "In My Country . . . "

The words in this chapter are used to describe people in the United States. What words do you use to describe people in your country?

3. Getting Personal

Newspapers often have ads, called "Personals," from people who are looking for romantic partners. Read the two Personal ads below. Ask your teacher to explain any vocabulary you do not understand. Then, write a Personal ad of your own. When you finish, share your ad with your classmates.

Young male professional (40—non-workaholic) looking for cute, brainy female (35-45) for relationship and possible marriage. Bilingual (French-English) and have traveled extensively. Emotionally stable. # 4673

Hispanic non-smoking vegetarian female (25) who likes astrology, massage, clean energy, jazz, and organic foods looking for like-minded male. # 8701

4. Survey

Ask five members of your class for the information in the chart below. When you finish, share your answers with your classmates.

Name	Describe your *favorite* kind of person. Give details.	What is your *least* favorite kind of person? Give details.
1.		
2.		
3.		
4.		
5.		

PEOPLE TRANSCRIPT

Helen and Mary, two high school seniors, are talking about their classmates.

Helen: Mary, are you still going out with Bob?

Mary: No Helen, I broke up with him because we're too different.

Helen: What do you mean?

Mary: Well . . . he's kind of a redneck.

Helen: Yeah, I know what you mean. His family lives out in the country. I'm surprised that they know what electricity is.

Mary: And he's always making rude jokes about my friends.

Helen: And he's always getting into fights!

Mary: Yeah, I'm tired of macho men.

Helen: Besides that he dresses like a slob!

Mary: He sure does.

Helen: How about Bill?

Mary: He's intelligent, but too much of a brain for me. He never does anything except read.

Helen: I think he's cute, but he doesn't like me.

Mary: Why don't you ask him out?

Helen: Rick wouldn't like that.

Mary: You're still going out with Rick?

Helen: Are you surprised?

Mary: Well, yes, a little bit. He's such a jock!

Helen: I like sports a lot. We play tennis every Saturday. (*pause*) By the way, Peter asked me out on a date yesterday.

Mary: Peter Jackson?

Helen: Yeah.

Mary: Yuck!!!

Helen: He is kind of a creep, isn't he?

Mary: I thought he was going steady with Betty.

Helen: She broke up with him!

Mary: Betty dumped Peter?

Helen: Yeah.

Mary: That's wonderful!

Helen: Uh-huh. So anyway, he asked me out and I told him, "No way."

Mary: Good for you!

Helen: He said that I was a snob.

Mary: A snob?

Helen: Yeah, can you believe it?

Mary: No, I can't! (*pause*) By the way, how's your brother Keith? Did he get into grad school?

Helen: Of course!! He's a brain. He studies all day every day. He's turned into such a nerd.

Mary: I think he's a sweetheart!

Helen: He's really intelligent, but he has zero social skills.

Mary: But he's such a nice guy!

Helen: Yeah, I guess so.

Mary: Is he still a vegetarian?

Helen: I think so. (*pause*) Hey, have you seen Matt lately?

Mary: You mean Mr. Perfect?

Helen: That's him.

Mary: No, I haven't, but I'd like to.

Helen: I know what you mean. He's fun to be around. He's a great conversationalist.

Mary: He's so much more mature than the other guys in this school.

Helen: And he's cute!

Mary: And he has a car!

Helen: Oh! What time do you have?

Mary: Six.

Helen: Oh, uh, I've got to go. I'll see you tomorrow. Let's walk to school together.

Mary: O.K. See you.

Helen: Bye.

CHAPTER FOURTEEN

CONVERSATIONAL EXPRESSIONS

LISTENING

In your country, when someone is talking about something that you no longer want to discuss, what can you say to change the subject?

Listen to each dialogue and fill in the blanks with T (true) or F (false). Listen again to check your answers.

1. Chris and Kevin are walking home from a pizza parlor.

_____ Chris and Kevin both thought that the vegetables were not fresh.

_____ Chris and Kevin agree that they won't have pizza again.

_____ They are worried because they left only a 5% tip for the waiter instead of 15%.

2. *A mother is trying to get her son, Todd, to help her.*

_____ Todd wants to help his mother.

_____ Todd has a lot of homework.

_____ Todd did the dishes the night before.

_____ The mother decides to do the dishes herself.

3. *Eric and Michael are talking.*

_____ Eric and Michael are good friends.

_____ Eric thinks that Michael likes Brenda.

_____ Suzie used to go out with Mark.

_____ Mark and Brenda went to a movie the night before.

_____ Eric wants Michael to ask Suzie out.

_____ Michael wanted to ask Suzie out in the past, but money was a problem.

_____ Eric owes Michael ten dollars.

_____ Eric and Marcie are going to the beach next weekend.

_____ Eric has an important chemistry test to take, so he has to leave.

FROM THE DIALOGUES

Study the vocabulary.

CONVERSATIONAL EXPRESSIONS

Actually is used to <u>correct</u> what someone has said.

> *Actually, you did them two days ago. (not last night!)*

By the way is used to <u>introduce</u> a new topic. It can mean, "I just thought of something."

> *By the way, how much did you leave as a tip?*
> *By the way, what were you doing at the Starlight Cinema?*

But can be used to <u>show disagreement</u>.

> *But I had to wash a bunch of dishes.*

Besides is used to <u>add a reason</u> to an argument.

> *Besides, I did them last night.*

What are you talking about? is used for <u>disagreement</u>. It can be used to say, "What do you mean?"

> A: *The vegetables weren't fresh.*
> B: *What're you talking about? They were fine.*

So what? can mean, "<u>Why</u> is this important?" or "<u>Why</u> are you telling me this?"

> A: *I saw Mark and Brenda out on the town last night!*
> B: *So what?*

That reminds me can mean, "What you just said <u>makes me remember</u> something."

> *That reminds me! Where's the five bucks you borrowed from me last week?*

Anyway is used to <u>end a main point</u> or to <u>return to a main point</u> already discussed. It is not used for a new point.

> *Anyway, we both agree to have the spaghetti next time.*
> *Anyway Michael, you have a chance with Suzie.*

Never mind is used to <u>end a topic</u> you do not want to talk about anymore. Also used is **Forget it**.

> *Never mind, I'll do them myself!*

VOCABULARY

bucks = dollars
disaster = a complete failure
tip = usually 15% extra is left in a restaurant as payment to the waiter

IDIOMS

a bunch of = many
out on the town = going out on a date (to a movie, dinner, dancing, etc.)
Don't blow it! = Don't fail!
Catch you later! = See you later!
Here you go. = used when giving something to someone.
to have a chance with = to have the opportunity to ask out on a date

CONVERSATION PRACTICE

1. Turn to page 142 and read the dialogues in pairs. Ask your teacher to explain any vocabulary or grammar you do not understand.

2. In the following conversation, circle the correct expression in parentheses. When you finish, read the conversation in pairs.

Ted: Hey Joan!

Joan: What's up?

Ted: Well, there's a big dance tonight at the Disco Palace!

Joan: Really? Who's playing?

Ted: The Sparklers.

Joan: I really like that place and I love the Sparklers!

Ted: Yeah, me too. (*Anyway / By the way*), I was wondering if you'd like to go with me tonight.

Joan: I'd love to. What time will you pick me up?

Ted: Around 8:00.

Joan: That sounds great! (*Anyway / By the way*), I saw your brother Tom last night.

Ted: (*So what? / What're you talking about?*)

Joan: You don't really like him, do you?

Ted: I don't know. I'd like him better if he'd get a job.

Joan: (*Never mind / Actually*), he's had several jobs in the last year.

Ted: Yeah, (*besides / but*) he always loses them.

Joan: You should try to be more understanding.

Ted: I've tried now for over 15 years.

Joan: (*Never mind / Actually*), we'll just get in an argument.

Ted: (*Anyway / That reminds me*), I'll come by about eight.

Joan: That sounds great.

Ted: Bye!

3. *Put the conversation in the correct order by numbering the sentences. The first one is done for you. When you finish, compare your answers with a classmate's answers.*

Two friends meet in a convenience store.

_____ Oh, that reminds me, she said she wanted to visit you soon. Should I call her and give her a message from you?

_____ She's doing better thanks. The operation was successful.

_____ Fine Mona. How've you been?

_____ Not on me, but I'll call you when I get home. (*pause*) Anyway, I'll be sure to give her yours.

_____ Not bad. Hey, how's your mother?

_____ Yeah, I'd better get home. It was nice seeing you.

_____ That would be great. (*pause*) Oh, never mind, I'll call her tomorrow myself. Do you have her number?

__1__ Bye.

_____ Hey Luis. How're you doing?

_____ Actually, I saw her yesterday. She's doing very well up in Seattle.

_____ I'd appreciate it. (*pause*) Well, it's getting late.

_____ I'm certainly glad to hear it. (*pause*) Oh, by the way, are you going to see Kathy next month?

_____ She is? I've been meaning to write to her.

YOUR TURN

1. Chit-Chat

Work in small groups. The teacher will give each member of the group two cards. Each card will have a conversational expression on it. Talk about one of the topics below.

> the weather
> last weekend
> music
> food
> school

During the conversation you must use the expressions on your cards. After you use the expression, throw the card in the middle of your group. The conversation must continue until everyone has thrown away their cards.

(Teachers: The cards for this exercise are on page 212 of the Appendix.)

Anyway, I'm glad you called.

CONVERSATIONAL EXPRESSIONS TRANSCRIPT

1. Chris and Kevin are walking home from a pizza parlor.

Kevin: Well, Chris. How was your pizza?

Chris: It was cold, but I don't mind cold pizza in the summer.

Kevin: Mine was a disaster! The pepperoni was too greasy.

Chris: But pepperoni is supposed to be greasy!

Kevin: No, it's not! And the vegetables weren't fresh.

Chris: What're you talking about? They were fine. The problem was that there wasn't enough cheese!

Kevin: Anyway, we both agree to have the spaghetti next time.

Chris: You can say that again! (*pause*) By the way, how much tip did you leave?

Kevin: I thought you left the tip!

Chris: Uh-oh. We'd better not go back there again.

2: A mother is trying to get her son, Todd, to help her.

Mother: You know Todd, it would really be nice if you did the dishes.

Todd: Aw, Mom. I've got three more pages of history to read and I have to write an essay for English class.

Mother: Washing the dishes would only take about 15 minutes.

Todd: But it's already 8:30! Besides, I did them last night. It's Betsy's turn.

Mother: Actually, you did them two days ago. Betsy did them last night.

Todd: But I had to wash a bunch of dishes. Betsy only had a few plates.

Mother: Never mind, I'll do them myself.

3: Eric and Michael are talking.

Eric: Hey Michael!

Michael: Hi Eric, what's up?

Eric: I saw Mark and Brenda out on the town last night!

Michael: So what?

Eric: Well, that means that Suzie was free.

Michael: Maybe she was with someone else.

Eric: Maybe she wasn't!

Michael: Where did you see Mark and Brenda?

Eric: At the Starlight Cinema.

Michael: Oh, yeah?

Eric: They were holding hands.

Michael: Are they going steady now?

Eric: Now how would I know that? (*pause*) Anyway Michael, now you have a chance with Suzie. Don't blow it like you did last time.

Michael: I didn't blow it last time! I just didn't have enough money to take her out anywhere! I've got a part-time job now.

Eric: That reminds me. Where's the five bucks you borrowed from me last week?

Michael: (*pulls out his wallet*) Here you go. (*pause*) By the way, what were you doing at the Starlight Cinema?

Eric: I had a date with Marcie.

Michael: Marcie? The blonde in our math class?

Eric: Yeah.

Michael: How'd that go?

Eric: Not bad, we're going to the beach on Saturday. Why don't you and Suzie come along?

Michael: Maybe we will!

Eric: Well, I've got to go to chemistry. I've got a big test to flunk!

Michael: I'll tell you if anything develops between Suzie and me.

Eric: O.K.! Catch you later!

Michael: Yeah!

CHAPTER FIFTEEN

FEELINGS

LISTENING

What puts you in a good mood? What puts you in a bad mood? Tell why.

Listen to the dialogue and fill in the blanks with T (true) or F (false). Listen again to check your answers.

Mark is talking to his counselor Dr. Smith, about his problems.

_____ Mark had a good relationship with his father.

_____ Mark's father was a very warm person.

_____ Mark's father was always working.

_____ Mark has a good relationship with his mother.

_____ Mark is from a small town.

_____ Mark has a low-paying job.

_____ Mark likes working with art galleries in his city.

_____ Mark does not like German Expressionism.

_____ Mark feels unhappy because he is alone.

_____ Mark likes the people in the city.

_____ Mark went through a red light and nearly ran into another car recently.

_____ Mark talked a lot about his sister.

FROM THE DIALOGUE

Study the vocabulary.

LIKES

I have **always loved** my mother deeply.
Even now, I'm **very close** to her.
We **get along** very well **with** each other.
I **really like** the feel**ing** of community.
I **really enjoy** help**ing** the local art museums.
I'm **really crazy about** German Expressionism.
I'm **interested in** getting more information about your relationship with your parents.

DISLIKES

I **never loved** my father.
I'm **sick and tired of** runn**ing** into so many selfish people!
I'm **bored by** small towns.
It is **difficult to** live alone.

ANGER

It **upsets me** and **makes me angry**!
It **made me so angry** that I wanted to kill him!

HURT FEELINGS / LONELINESS

He **never paid any attention to** me and that **hurt my feelings**.
Well, I'm **lonely** here.
I **get homesick for** small town life. (I miss small town life.)

WORRIES / PROBLEMS

It **is difficult to** live alone.
Sometimes I **have trouble** sleep**ing**.
I'm **worried** about the lack of culture.

IDIOMS

I consider myself a small town kind of person. = I think that I am a small town kind of person.
How do you feel about your mother? = What do you think about your mother?
Listen carefully to **her side of the story** = Listen carefully to her point of view.

VOCABULARY

cold = does not show his feelings
workaholic = is always working; never has any fun
intimate = people are close or friendly to each other
jerk = a bad or stupid person
yelled = said in a very loud voice

CONVERSATION PRACTICE

1. Turn to page 149 and read the dialogue in pairs. Ask your teacher to explain any vocabulary or grammar you do not understand.

Loneliness

2. Complete each sentence. Match the first part of each sentence in Column One with the second part of the sentence in Column Two.

Column One

_____ I'm crazy about . . .

_____ I really get along with . . .

_____ I'm sick and tired of . . .

_____ I really enjoy going . . .

_____ I'm really worried that . . .

_____ I'm really interested in going to . . .

_____ I'm really bored by people who . . .

_____ It made me angry that he . . .

_____ My brother never paid . . .

_____ It hurt my feelings that . . .

_____ I'm very close to all of my . . .

_____ I get homesick . . .

_____ I consider myself . . .

_____ I get lonely when I live . . .

_____ It is difficult to . . .

_____ In school, I have trouble . . .

_____ It upsets me when my father says . . .

_____ I'm sick and tired of working . . .

Column Two

a. to visit my brother.

b. he said I was fat.

c. six days a week.

d. people throwing garbage on our street.

e. attention to me.

f. I'm lazy.

g. passing tests.

h. my mother.

i. when I think of my family back in Colombia.

j. chocolate ice cream.

k. save money.

l. family.

m. alone.

n. the beach.

o. are always talking about themselves.

p. a big-city person.

q. there will be a war.

r. hit my sister.

YOUR TURN

1. *In small groups, finish the following sentences with information from your life. Then share your answers with your group.*

I'm worried about . . .

1. I'm very close to _____ .
2. I get along very well with _____ .
3. I consider myself _____ .
4. I really like (verb+*ing*) _____ .
5. It's very important for me to _____ .
6. I'm worried about _____
7. I am bored by _____ .
8. I really enjoy (verb+*ing*) _____ .
9. I'm really crazy about _____ .
10. It is difficult to _____ .
11. I have trouble (verb+*ing*) _____ .
12. _____ upsets me.
13. _____ makes me angry.
14. I'm sick and tired of _____ .

2. Survey

Ask five members of your class for the information in the chart below. When you finish, discuss your answers with your classmates.

Name	Describe in complete sentences the thing you like most in life.	Describe in complete sentences the thing you dislike most in life.	What makes you angry? Describe in detail one time that you got angry.
1.			
2.			
3.			
4.			
5.			

FEELINGS TRANSCRIPT

Mark is talking to his counselor, Dr. Smith, about his problems.

Mark: I never loved my father.

Dr. Smith: Why not?

Mark: Well, I disliked him because he was such a cold man.

Dr. Smith: Really?

Mark: Yes. . . . And he was rarely at home. He was a workaholic. (*pause*) He never paid any attention to me and that hurt my feelings.

Dr. Smith: How do you feel about your mother?

Mark: I have always loved my mother deeply.

Dr. Smith: Uh-huh.

Mark: Even now, I'm very close to her. We get along very well with each other.

Dr. Smith: Where is she now?

Mark: She still lives in the same small town that we lived in when I was a child.

Dr. Smith: How often do you see her?

Mark: I go down there about once a month.

Dr. Smith: Uh-huh.

Mark: I call her once or twice a month. Sometimes I get homesick for small town life.

Dr. Smith: Why is that?

Mark: Because life is more intimate. People really know you. I still have many close friends there. I consider myself a small town kind of person.

Dr. Smith: What does that mean exactly?

Mark: It means that I really like the feeling of community and tradition that people in small towns have.

Dr. Smith: Why don't you move back there?

Mark: There's no work. Here in the big city I earn a lot of money. It's very important for me to have a good-paying job.

Dr. Smith: I understand.

Mark: Besides, I'm worried about the lack of culture. Sometimes I'm bored by small towns.

Dr. Smith: For example?

Mark: Here in the city, I really enjoy helping the local art museums and art galleries.

Dr. Smith: What kind of art do you like?

Mark: Well, I'm really crazy about German Expressionism.

Dr. Smith: It sounds like you have an active social life and a good job. What exactly is your problem?

Mark: Well, I'm lonely here. I don't have a wife or girlfriend. I live alone.

Dr. Smith: It is difficult to live alone.

Mark: Sometimes I have trouble sleeping.

Dr. Smith: Really.

Mark: Yeah, sometimes I don't sleep well for two or three days in a row.

Dr. Smith: That must be very difficult.

Mark: Yeah. Also, I think that people are really rude here. It upsets me and makes me angry!

Dr. Smith: Can you give me an example?

Mark: Sure. The other day I was driving downtown when this jerk ran a red light and nearly killed me. Then he honked his horn and yelled at me! It made me so angry that I wanted to kill him! I'm sick and tired of running into so many selfish people.

Dr. Smith: That's certainly understandable. (*pause*) Well, Mark, our time's up for today.

Mark: It went really fast!

Dr. Smith: It usually does. (*pause*) You're going to visit your mother in the country this weekend, aren't you?

Mark: Yes.

Dr. Smith: While you are there, I'd like you to think about what you've said today. It's been a good beginning, but I need more details.

Mark:	For example?
Dr. Smith:	You have said nothing about your relationship with your sister. Also, I'm interested in getting more information about your relationship with your parents.
Mark:	Uh-huh.
Dr. Smith:	I want you to sit down with your mother this weekend and have a long talk.
Mark:	O.K.
Dr. Smith:	Tell her how you feel about your father and listen carefully to her side of the story. We'll talk about it next week. That's enough for now.
Mark:	Thank you doctor.
Dr. Smith:	It's my pleasure. I'll see you next week.
Mark:	Bye.

CONVERSATION MAZE TWO

CONVERSATION MAZE TWO

Read the section marked *Situation*. Ask your teacher to explain any vocabulary or grammar you do not understand. Then, read the question and choose one of the possible answers (*A, B,* or *C*). Each answer will send you to a new numbered section. Go to the number indicated and read the *Explanation*. If you choose the best answer, the *Situation* will continue and another question will be asked. If you did not choose the best answer, you will be instructed to return to the previous section and try again. Continue through the maze until you have ended the conversation.

When you are reading one section, you may **not** look at any other section.

SITUATION

You are Bob. You have known Mary for about six years. You share several interests including hiking, skiing, and going to movies. There is no romance involved, just friendship.

You are meeting Mary and her friend Remi for dinner. Mary has told you only that Remi is French and that she met him when she did a homestay in southern France ten years ago. Remi and Mary walk up to you in front of Chez Moi, a famous French restaurant.

What should you say?

   A. (*Because you don't know Remi, wait for an introduction. Mary will introduce you.*) ➡ Go to **14**.

   B. Good evening. (*Look at both of them. Mary will introduce you to Remi.*) ➡ Go to **20**.

   C. Hi Remi. ➡ Go to **7**.

---

1 **EXPLANATION:** This is much too short. You should give a complete answer. ➡ Return to **24**.

---

2 **EXPLANATION:** This comment is too simple. It doesn't give Remi and Mary anything to say in response. ➡ Return to **23**.

---

3 **EXPLANATION:** This is the best answer because it responds to Remi's opening and it makes another step in the conversation.

   Remi says, "Yes, that's right." (*Before he can continue, Mary takes the two of you into the restaurant. A waiter then takes you to a reserved table. After ordering, you settle down and begin talking. Your goal: a pleasant conversation.*)

   Which of the following do you think would be the best opener?

      A. Nice weather we've been having, don't you think? ➡ Go to **21**.

      B. Uh, Remi, what part of France do you live in? ➡ Go to **32**.

      C. Do you like to go to movies? ➡ Go to **19**.

---

4 **EXPLANATION:** This only addresses half of what Remi said —*schools*. You also need to address what was said about *students*. ➡ Return to **27**.

---

5 EXPLANATION: This is the best answer because it gives Remi something interesting to respond to —*politics*.

Mary says, "Bob just wrote an article about American education."
Remi says, "Oh, really?"

What should you say?

> A. Yes, I said that American education is quite good in its philosophy, but students don't work hard enough. ➡ Go to **27**.

> B. Yes, I wrote about the problems in American schools. ➡ Go to **35**.

> C. Yes, I wrote about the problems and strengths of American education. I think that it's a serious question in America today. We really need to think about it carefully. ➡ Go to **29**.

6 EXPLANATION: This is a closed question, so it does not help the conversation develop as well as an open question. ➡ Return to **23**.

7 EXPLANATION: Before using his name, you should be introduced or at least say, "You must be Remi." ➡ Return to the **beginning situation**.

8 EXPLANATION: This is the best answer because it develops the conversation by asking Remi for more information. It is more than just a comment.

Remi says, "Bentel does large civil engineering projects like dams, bridges, highways and large buildings. I'm a systems analyst. I work with their architects in the building design section."

You do not know what a systems analyst is. What do you say?

> A. Excuse me, but I don't know what a systems analyst does exactly. Is it related to computers? ➡ Go to **24**.

> B. You're a systems . . . ? ➡ Go to **17**.

> C. What does a systems analyst do? ➡ Go to **33**.

9 EXPLANATION: This is much too short. ➡ Return to **32**.

10 EXPLANATION: You should give more information about writing. Answering the telephone is not the interesting part of the job. ➡ Return to **24**.

11 EXPLANATION: This does not logically follow what Remi said. He made a statement about France. ➡ Return to **27**.

12 EXPLANATION: This doesn't help the conversation develop. ➡ Return to **20**.

13 EXPLANATION: Nice is too weak. ➡ Return to **31**.

14 EXPLANATION: It is better to show that you are interested in meeting someone new. Don't wait for an introduction. ➡ Return to the beginning situation.

15 EXPLANATION: This is a very long reply, but it really says nothing. It doesn't give Remi anything to say in response. ➡ Return to **32**.

16 EXPLANATION: This is a good paraphrase of what was said. It should encourage Remi to continue.

He says, "Yes, that's exactly what I think. It's much too restrictive. The students have no freedom." (*The waiter arrives with the food and the three of you begin eating. There is silence for a fairly long time. Finally, all three of you seem ready to resume the conversation. You would like to open a new topic—France.*)

Which of the following is the best opener?

> A. Anyway, how about France? ⇒ Go to **36**.
>
> B. I'd love to go to France! ⇒ Go to **23**.
>
> C. By the way, I'm hoping to go to France someday. ⇒ Go to **25**.

17 EXPLANATION: This is much too vague. It doesn't tell the speaker what was not understood. ⇒ Return to **8**.

18 EXPLANATION: This is the best answer because wonderful matches Remi's word splendid well.

While he is talking, the waiter brings the check. The three of you divide the cost and head towards the door. Outside, Remi says, "It was very nice talking to you."

What is the best response?

> A. Yes, I'm really enjoying our conversation. What places outside of Paris should I try to see? ⇒ Go to **34**.
>
> B. I hope that I'll see you again. Good-bye. ⇒ Go to **28**.
>
> C. Yes, I really enjoyed our conversation. I hope that we'll be able to meet again. ⇒ Go to **26**.

19 EXPLANATION: It's too soon to talk about this. First, you need to find out some personal information about Remi. ⇒ Return to **3**.

20 EXPLANATION: This is the best response because you are showing interest in beginning a relationship with Remi by looking at him and greeting him along with Mary.

Mary says, "Remi, I'd like you to meet my good friend, Bob."
Remi looks at you and says, "I've been looking forward to meeting you."

What should you say and do?

> A. It's nice to meet you, too. Mary has told me a great deal about you. (*Move toward Remi and extend your arm for a handshake.*) ⇒ Go to **30**.
>
> B. It's a pleasure to meet you. (*Move toward Remi.*) ⇒ Go to **12**.
>
> C. I've been looking forward to meeting you, too. Mary told me she met you in France. (*Move toward Remi and extend your arm for a handshake.*) ⇒ Go to **3**.

21 EXPLANATION: Talking about the weather is more normal as a conversational opener with someone you already know. ⇒ Return to **3**.

22 EXPLANATION: This is O.K., but you should show more enthusiasm. There is a better answer. ⇒ Return to **31**.

23 **EXPLANATION:** This is the best response. It invites Remi or Mary to ask you why you would like to go.

> Remi asks you, "Why would you like to go to France?"
> You reply, "I studied French in high school and was impressed by the beautiful illustrations in my book."
> Mary says, "Really?"
> You continue, "I've loved French painting for years."
> Remi says, "I recommend that you start in Paris. It's the most beautiful city in France."

What is the best response?

> A. Should I see Notre Dame? ➟ Go to **6**.
>
> B. What should I see or do in Paris? ➟ Go to **31**.
>
> C. That's a good idea. ➟ Go to **2**.

24 **EXPLANATION:** This is the best answer because it is specific.

> Remi looks at you and says, "Yes, that's right. I work with computer programs, designing them, writing them, and correcting problems. (**pause**) Remi continues, "Mary says that you're a writer for a newspaper."

What should you say?

> A. Actually, I'm only a part-time writer. I spend most of my time answering telephone calls from customers. They want to subscribe or they want information. ➟ Go to **10**.
>
> B. Yes, I work for a small newspaper covering local and statewide politics. Most of the time, though, I answer the telephone. ➟ Go to **5**.
>
> C. Actually, I'm only a part-time writer. ➟ Go to **1**.

25 **EXPLANATION:** *By the way* is not appropriate here. It is usually used to mean, *I just remembered something important that I need to tell you/ask you.* ➟ Return to **16**.

26 **EXPLANATION:** This is an appropriate pre-closing.

> Remi says, "When you come to Paris, come visit me."
> You say, "I'll do that! And next time you come to the U.S., please contact me."Remi says, "I will."

(The three of you say good-bye.)

27 **EXPLANATION:** This is a good answer because it specifically tells about what you wrote. Remi and Mary can now comment on *philosophy* or *students*.

> Mary says, "I agree with you. I think that our system encourages students to be independent, but the social problems hurt them."
> Remi says, "I think that the opposite is true in France."

What would be a good follow up to this?

> A. Yes, we certainly have severe social problems in the U.S. ➟ Go to **11**.
>
> B. Are the schools poor in France? ➟ Go to **4**.
>
> C. So you think that in France the system is poor, but the students are working hard? ➟ Go to **16**.

28 **EXPLANATION:** This is too abrupt. The good-bye should come after more pre-closings. ➟ Return to **18**.

29 EXPLANATION: This is too vague. It says nothing. ⟶ Return to **5**.

30 EXPLANATION: This sounds strange because Mary has not told you a lot about Remi. ⟶ Return to **20**.

31 EXPLANATION: This is an open question, so it develops the conversation well.

Remi talks at some length about his favorite places in Paris. At one point he says, "The architecture is especially splendid!"

You want to encourage his enthusiasm. What could you say?

      A. It sounds wonderful! ⟶ Go to **18**.

      B. Really? ⟶ Go to **22**.

      C. It really sounds very nice! ⟶ Go to **13**.

32 EXPLANATION: This is the best answer. When you have just met someone it's normal to begin the conversation by finding out *personal information*. In this situation, questions such as, *Where are you from?*, *What do you do?*, and *Where are you living?* sound very natural.

(*Remi looks over at you and smiles.*) He says, "I live in Paris because I'm working for the Bentel Corporation. Their headquarters in France is in Paris."

Which is the best reply?

      A. I've never been to Paris, but I'd really love to go. I've heard so much about it that I've thought about going there for a long time. ⟶ Go to **15**.

      B. Oh, really? ⟶ Go to **9**.

      C. Really? (*pause*) I don't know anything about the Bentel Corporation. What do you do for them? ⟶ Go to **8**.

33 EXPLANATION: This is better than B, but still not as specific as A. If you say this, he will think you know nothing about computers. ⟶ Return to **8**.

34 EXPLANATION: Remi is trying to end the conversation. He does not want you to begin a new topic. ⟶ Return to **18**.

35 EXPLANATION: This is much too short. You should try to give a complete answer. ⟶ Return to **5**.

36 EXPLANATION: This sounds too abrupt. *Anyway* is best for a situation in which you have strayed off the topic or want to conclude a topic. You want to start a new topic. ⟶ Return to **16**.

CHAPTER SIXTEEN

STORYTELLING

LISTENING

When you don't understand something in English, what do you do? Stay silent? Ask a question? Nod your head?

Listen to the dialogue and fill in the blanks with T (true) or F (false). Listen again to check your answers.

Mary is telling her grandson, Bobby, about his father's childhood.

_____ This story happens around 1975.

_____ It takes place in the Appalachian Mountains.

_____ The Appalachian Mountains are on the West Coast of the United States.

_____ Three people went on the camping trip.

_____ They left at about 6 o'clock in the evening.

_____ After a hike of about two days, they stopped in a forest.

_____ In the middle of the night, they heard a loud noise.

_____ Then, they saw a mountain lion.

_____ The boys ran home; it took them about a day and a half.

HOW TO TELL A STORY

When you begin telling a story, be sure to give a complete background:

        A. What is the story about?

        B. When and where did it take place?

        C. Generally, what was the situation?

Examples: **A.** This is a story about your father. **B.** Once when he was 15, **C.** he went hiking with friends.

        A. I have something important to tell you about your father. **B.** In Virginia about 3 years ago, **C.** he saved a man's life.

        A. This story is about my early life. **B.** About ten years ago in Alaska, **C.** I had a terrible experience.

        A. I had an interesting experience **B.** when I was in Beijing. **C.** I met a 93-year-old woman who had been a servant for the last Emperor of China.

FROM THE DIALOGUE

Study the vocabulary.

BEGINNING A STORY—BACKGROUND

This story is about a camping trip.
It takes place around 1965 when he was about 15 years old.
During summer vacation, your father went hiking in the Appalachian Mountains.

LISTENER EXPRESSIONS FOR STORIES

Go on!
What did Dad **do?**
What did the bear **do?**
What did they **do?**
What happened after that?
What happened then?

TIME EXPRESSIONS

That was a long time **ago**.
after eating one of my excellent breakfasts.
after they had been hiking for about two days . . . (after + i*ng*)
after it had finished eating the food . . .
then before going to sleep . . . (before + i*ng*)
then, they got so scared . . .
Finally, they decided . . .
How long did it **take** them to get home?

IDIOMS
---

it **got** really angry (got = became)
they got **so scared that** . . . (so + adjective + that)
to **get** home (to **arrive** home)

CONVERSATION PRACTICE

1. *Turn to page 163 and read the dialogue in pairs. Ask your teacher to explain any vocabulary or grammar you do not understand.*

2. *Complete each sentence by matching Column One to Column Two. The first one is done for you.*

Column One	Column Two
__e__ Once when he was about 15,	a. at about 6 o'clock in the morning.
_____ He was with two friends	b. about a day and a half to get home.
_____ They left	c. began moving toward them.
_____ After they had been hiking for about two days,	d. they ran to the nearest tree and climbed up it.
_____ They put up their tents, ate dinner, and went right to sleep	e. he went hiking in the Appalachian Mountains.
_____ In the middle of the night,	f. and calmly ate it.
_____ They began yelling and banging their pots together	g. they stopped for the night in a thick forest.
_____ The bear got really angry and	h. down the tree and run home.
_____ They got so scared that	i. because they were so tired.
_____ The bear went back to the food	j. from his high school.
_____ After the bear had finished eating the food,	k. they heard a big noise outside near the campfire.
_____ He and his friends	l. waited a while.
_____ Finally, they decided to quietly climb	m. to scare the bear off.
_____ It took them	n. it went to sleep.

3. *Put the conversation in the correct order by numbering the sentences. The first one is done for you.*

_____ On 40, I got a ride with a college student for a day and a half.

_____ Then, in Tennessee I headed west on Highway 40.

_____ We had a good time together, but he finally had to drop me off in New Mexico.

_____ The first day, I started going up to Tennessee from Florida.

_____ He took me across the Mississippi River and through most of the West.

_____ Two days later, I finally got to San Francisco.

__1__ When I was 21, I hitchhiked from Florida to California.

4. *Fill in the blanks with the appropriate phrases.*

did she do	then	really	about
got	after	takes place	anyway

A: This is a story _____ your mother.

B: Oh good! I love stories about her.

A: It _____ during World War II.

B: When was that?

A: The United States entered the war in 1941. (*pause*) _____ , your mother joined the Women's Army Corps.

B: She was a soldier!

A: Yes, she was. She drove trucks all over the United States.

B: _____ ?

A: Uh-huh. And one day she was driving through Kentucky and she saw an automobile accident.

B: What _____ ?

A: She jumped out of her truck.

B: Uh-huh.

A: And _____ opening one of the car doors, she pulled a woman and a child out of the car.

B: Great!

A: _____ , the car started burning about one minute after she _____ them out.

B: So she was a hero!

A: Yeah.

YOUR TURN

*In small groups, take turns telling a story by answering <u>one</u> of the questions below. Remember to begin by telling what the story is about and when/where it happened. Use proper time expressions. Listeners should use appropriate listener responses (**Uh-huh, Really! What happened after that? What did you do then?**).*

1. What is the most exciting, dangerous, or interesting experience that you have ever had? When did it take place? Where did it happen? Describe it step-by-step.

2. What is the saddest experience that you have ever had?

3. Tell the story of a movie or television program you saw recently.

Write the first two sentences of your story in the blanks below.

_____

_____

_____

_____

_____

My most dangerous experience.

STORYTELLING TRANSCRIPT

Mary is telling her grandson, Bobby, about his father's childhood.

Mary: Your father was very adventurous when he was younger.

Bobby: Are you serious?

Mary: Of course I'm serious. He was always getting into trouble.

Bobby: What kind of trouble?

Mary: Well . . . I can tell you a story that's a good example.

Bobby: O.K.

Mary: Of course, if you're not really interested . . .

Bobby: No, I really want to hear it!

Mary: All right. This story is about a camping trip. It takes place around 1965 when he was about 15 years old.

Bobby: That was a long time ago!

Mary: Yes, it was. During summer vacation, your father went hiking in the Appalachian Mountains.

Bobby: Where's that?

Mary: Umm . . .they're on the East Coast.

Bobby: The East Coast?

Mary: Yes, in Virginia. Didn't you learn this in school?

Bobby: No, but I know where Virginia is. I was born there.

Mary: Well, I'm glad that you know that at least. (*pause*) Now, where was I? Oh, yes. He was with two friends from his high school. And, uh . . . they left at about 6 o'clock in the morning after eating one of my excellent breakfasts.

Bobby: Only three people?

Mary: Well, let me think a moment. Yes, that's right. I'm sure it was only three.

Bobby: Weren't they afraid to go in such a small group?

Mary: Your, uh, father didn't worry much when he was young. (*pause*) Anyway, one night, after they had been hiking for about two days, they stopped for the night in a thick forest.

Bobby: Uh-oh.

Mary: What's wrong?

Bobby: It sounds like something bad is going to happen.

Mary: You're right. They put up their tents and ate dinner.

Bobby: Uh-huh.

Mary: And then before going to sleep, they put all of their food in a large bag and hid it in a tree.

Bobby: What happened after that?

Mary: Well, in the middle of the night, they heard a big noise outside near that same tree. (*pause*)

Bobby: Go on! What was the noise?

Mary: Well, they rushed out of their tents.

Bobby: Uh-huh.

Mary: And there was a gigantic black bear in the tree eating all of their food.

Bobby: What did they do?

Mary: They began yelling and banging their pots together to scare the bear off.

Bobby: What did the bear do?

Mary: Well, it got really angry. It came down from the tree and then began moving toward them.

Bobby: What happened then?

Mary: Then, they got so scared that they ran to another tree and climbed up it.

Bobby: What did the bear do?

Mary: It went back to the food and calmly ate it.

Bobby: That's terrible!

Mary: Yes it was. (*pause*) After it had finished eating the food, it went to sleep.

Bobby: What did Dad do?

Mary: Well, he and his friends waited a while. Finally, they decided to quietly climb down the tree and run home.

Bobby: How long did it take them to get home?

Mary: About a day and a half.

Bobby: With no food?

Mary: Your father was quite tough when he was young.

Bobby: Really?

Mary: Really.

CHAPTER SEVENTEEN

LIFE

LISTENING

Are your grandparents living? If not, do you remember them? Can you recall two or three interesting stories they told you about their lives?

Listen to the dialogue and fill in the blanks with T (true) or F (false). Listen again to check your answers.

Bobby is asking his grandmother Mary about her life.

_____ Mary is 66 years old.

_____ She was born in Pasco County in Florida.

_____ Mary loved living in Florida.

_____ Mary had to quit school after the 6th grade because her family was poor.

_____ She worked in a hardware store.

_____ Mary got married when she was 21 years old.

_____ Mary's husband Joseph was an excellent dancer and a handsome man.

_____ Mary and Joseph were married for five years.

_____ Mary became a widow.

_____ After some time, Mary married another man.

_____ Mary's second husband was a very interesting man.

_____ Mary and her second husband adopted a child.

_____ Mary left her second husband after two years.

_____ Bobby asks his grandmother a very personal question about her love affairs.

_____ Mary began working at the water company.

_____ Mary enjoyed working.

_____ Mary's sister Susan got a divorce and moved in with her.

FROM THE DIALOGUE

Study the vocabulary.

PEOPLE IN LIFE

an adopted baby = someone else's baby taken in and raised as part of the family
an alcoholic = a person addicted to alcohol
a widow = a woman whose husband has died (man = **widower**)

GENERAL QUESTIONS: LIFE

When were you born?   **I was born** 76 years ago in Pasco County.
How old were you?   **I was** 13 at the time.

GOOD EVENTS

to get married / to marry = to take a wife or husband
to remarry = to marry again
a wedding anniversary = the day on which a wedding took place in an earlier year
to move = to go to live in a new place
to move in with = to come to live with
to get a job (to get = to receive)
to get promoted = to be given a more important job
to retire = to stop working, usually at the age of 65

> **NOTE:** *got + married* or *divorced* does
> <u>not</u> take an object
> (a person's name).
> Compare:
> I married Sue. → I got married.
> I divorced Bill. → I got divorced.

BAD EVENTS

to die young
to die in an automobile accident
to never marry again
to get divorced = to end a marriage
the Great Depression = the terrible time from 1929 to about 1940; many people were
homeless or hungry.

IDIOMS

a love affair = a romantic relationship
roots = where a family came from
to get by = to survive
to grow up = to become an adult
to raise two children = to take care of two children

CONVERSATION PRACTICE

1. Turn to page 171 and read the dialogue in pairs. Ask your teacher to explain any vocabulary or grammar you do not understand.

2. Put the sentences in the correct order by numbering them. The first one is done for you.

_____ In 1990, my wife finished law school.

_____ I lived in Erie until I was six.

_____ I grew up there.

_____ She got a job with a well-known law firm; her salary paid the tuition for my M.A. in Literature.

_____ We still love each other very much and will stay together for the rest of our lives.

___1___ I was born in Erie, Pennsylvania in 1952.

_____ After graduating from high school, I went to work on a fishing boat.

_____ Two years after our marriage, my wife got pregnant with our first child; our second child was born two years after that.

_____ We fell in love and after a six-month romance, we became engaged.

_____ Then, we moved to Texas. I went to elementary school in Dallas.

_____ In 1964, my dad got a job in Seattle, Washington.

_____ Working on a boat was too difficult for me and not very satisfying. So in 1976, I entered the University of Washington.

_____ We plan to travel after we retire and spend the rest of our golden years playing with our grandchildren.

_____ Her name was Joanne. She was majoring in pre-law.

_____ In my junior year, I met a wonderful woman.

_____ I majored in American literature.

_____ After being engaged for six months, we got married.

YOUR TURN

1. Interview

In pairs, interview a partner using the questions below. After each question, ask a follow-up question (an open question which gives you more information). The interviewer should use listener expressions.

Interview Questions

Where were you born?
Where did you grow up?
How many different places have you lived in?
Where were they?
What schools have you gone to?
What did you study/major in?
Have you ever fallen in love?
Are you married? Have you ever been married/divorced?
Do you have any children? How many?
What would you like to do when you retire?

Example: A: Where did you grow up? (*question*)
B: In Berlin. (*answer*)
A: Really? How did you like Berlin? (*follow-up question*)

Other follow-up questions

What did you think about _____ ?
What was _____ like?
Why did you _____ ?

When you finish the interview, give a short presentation about your partner's life to the class.

2. Homework

Visit, write, or telephone one of your older relatives and interview him/her about his/her life. Ask them about the following:

- birth
- childhood
- marriage
- employment
- travel
- children
- retirement

When you have finished gathering information, give a detailed report to your class about your relative's life.

3. In My Country . . .

In small groups, answer the following questions about your country. Be prepared to discuss your answers with the class.

What is the youngest age that people can get married?

Is the general divorce rate high or low? Is it easy or difficult to get a divorce in your country?

How do marriage partners in your country usually meet? Is there a system of arranged marriages? Are there singles bars/newspapers?

About how many children do people have? Is it normal to have large or small families?

If there is time, answer these further questions about your country.

How long does the average person live in your country? What factors affect life expectancy?

Approximately what percentage of men/women smoke cigarettes?

Do people in your country drink alcoholic beverages? What kind? How much?

What is the most common cause of death in your country?

What percentage of people in your country graduate from high school? from university?

Do people in your country move a great deal or do they stay in the same area?

At what age do people retire? What do people do after they have retired? Are there retirement homes/cities? Do they live with their families or in separate housing?

4. My First Memory

What is the first thing that you remember in your life? Tell the class. Give as many details as you can.

5. If . . .

Ask students who they would trade lives with if they could.

LIFE TRANSCRIPT

Bobby is asking his grandmother Mary about her life.

Bobby: Grandma, when were you born?

Mary: My! You are curious today, aren't you?

Bobby: I just want to know about our family. Dad says it's important to know your roots.

Mary: I was born 76 years ago in Pasco County in Florida.

Bobby: Florida? That must have been wonderful!

Mary: It was miserable! There was no air conditioning and we didn't have screens on the windows to keep out the insects.

Bobby: That's too bad. (*pause*) Did you grow up there?

Mary: Yes, I went to a very small school there until 6th grade when I got my first job. My family was very poor and we needed the money.

Bobby: How old were you?

Mary: I was 13 at the time. I worked in a grocery store as a clerk and cleaning lady.

Bobby: How long did you work there?

Mary: Well, let me see. I worked there through my teens. At the age of 20, I quit my job and I married your grandfather, Joseph Sylvester Frey.

Bobby: Wow! It sounds as if life was difficult!

Mary: It was at times. I wish that I had had more time for fun while I was a teenager. Your grandfather was the one who finally taught me how to enjoy myself.

Bobby: Really?

Mary: Yes, he was an excellent dancer and very handsome, like you and your father.

Bobby: Did I ever meet him?

Mary: No, he died young. He died soon after our fifth wedding anniversary.

Bobby: So you were a widow?

Mary: Yes, I became a widow at the age of 25. I had two children, your father was the oldest.

Bobby: What did you do?

Mary: We moved to Virginia to live with my cousins. Eventually, I remarried.

Bobby: What was your second husband like?

Mary: He was a very kind, but boring man. He liked to sit home and read the newspaper.

Bobby: I'm sorry.

Mary: Don't be sorry. He was a hard worker and he helped me take care of my baby Sarah and your father. And then we adopted a baby from one of his relatives.

Bobby: What happened to that baby?

Mary: That poor child died with my husband in an automobile accident. We had only been married for two years when it happened. (*pause*) I never got married again.

Bobby: Did you have any love affairs?

Mary: Teenagers are so rude these days! You shouldn't ask such questions!

Bobby: Sorry Grandma. What did you do after your second husband died?

Mary: Well, I got a job at the phone company and worked there until I retired.

Bobby: Did you like your job?

Mary: Oh, let me see. Actually, I would rather have spent more time with my children, but the money was good after I got promoted to supervisor.

Bobby: I guess it was difficult raising two children and working.

Mary: Yes, but during the Great Depression and 40s we all lived in one big house, so there were plenty of people to help. My sister Susan got a divorce from her alcoholic husband, so she moved in with us.

Bobby: Uh, was it crowded?

Mary: Yes, it was very crowded, but we always managed to get by. Families survive bad times if they stick together. That's the lesson you should remember. (*pause*) And now, it's time for you to go to bed, young man.

Bobby: Oh, Grandma! Do I have to?

Mary: Yes, you have to. Now, give me a kiss on the cheek and off you go to bed.

Bobby: Good night and thanks for the story.

Mary: You're very welcome. It was my pleasure, believe me. Now, if I could just remember where I left my eyeglasses.

CHAPTER EIGHTEEN

WORK

LISTENING

> Do you work now? Do you like your job? Do you like the people you work with? Why or why not?

Listen to the dialogue and fill in the blanks with T (true) or F (false). Listen again to check your answers.

Two business people, Mika and Arthur, are talking about their jobs over lunch.

_____ Arthur really likes his job.

_____ Arthur and his boss get along very well.

_____ Arthur always agrees with his boss.

_____ Arthur says that his boss needs him too much to fire him.

_____ Arthur has applied to Integrated Technologies for a new job.

_____ Arthur knows a lot about computers.

_____ Integrated Technologies hired a lot of people last year.

_____ Integrated Technologies' pay is very good, but their benefits are not very good.

_____ Employees of Integrated Technologies get four weeks of paid vacation and good medical insurance.

_____ Integrated Technologies has a good reputation for its treatment of women and minorities.

_____ Arthur is black (African-American).

_____ Arthur rarely works overtime.

_____ Arthur likes his colleagues at work.

_____ Mika does not like her boss.

_____ Mika's boss loves his family.

_____ Mika's boss insists that everyone take vacations.

_____ Mika's boss complains about her work.

_____ Mika's company needs someone in the Personnel Department.

FROM THE DIALOGUE

Study the vocabulary.

LOSING A JOB

fire = to dismiss a worker; the person does not want to stop working

quit = a worker leaves a job; the worker wants to stop working

lay off = to dismiss a worker because business is bad

incompetent = has no ability

GETTING A JOB

Why don't you apply for other jobs? = to look for a new job

hiring = giving jobs to new employees

Personnel = the department of a company that hires and fires employees (workers). It also keeps employee records and controls benefits.

minority = a racial or ethnic group of people that makes up a small percentage (%) of the American people

JOB BENEFITS

benefits = for example: medical insurance, vacation pay, sick pay

bonus = money given for good performance

daycare = a place which takes care of children

holidays = special days when companies close (for example: Christmas, New Year's Day, Thanksgiving, July 4th)

medical coverage = insurance that pays for all or most of the bill if you are sick

OTHER JOB VOCABULARY

promotion = a move to a better job in the same company

raise in pay = more money

transferred from . . . to . . . = moved to a different part of the same company

IDIOMS

branch office = an office of the company that is not as important as the headquarters (the main office)

the grapevine = an informal system of communication from person to person

overtime = work that is over 8 hours per day or 40 hours per week.

paperwork = writing reports, filling out papers

stab everyone else **in the back** = to hurt each other

CONVERSATION PRACTICE

1. *Turn to page 179 and read the dialogue in pairs. Ask your teacher to explain any vocabulary or grammar you do not understand.*

2. *Complete each sentence with the correct word or phrase.*

the grapevine

benefits	overtime	promotion	quit	fired

1. If you work 48 hours one week, you will have 8 hours of _____ .

2. In my company, employees receive 4 weeks of vacation , 2 weeks of sick leave, full medical, and dental coverage and 11 holidays per year. I think that the _____ are quite good.

3. Arthur was _____ from his job because he stole some money.

4. Mary _____ her job because she didn't like her boss.

5. June got a _____ because she did such excellent work.

on the grapevine	hiring	raise	laid off	bonus

6. Harry got a $2000 a year _____ because he's a good worker.

7. Joan got a $1000 _____ in March because of his work on a special project.

8. Intercorp Inc. is _____ people for their Personnel Department.

9. Business was very slow last year, so some companies _____ workers.

10. I heard about your transfer _____ .

minorities	paperwork	apply for	headquarters	transferred

11. Jack was _____ from Miami to San Francisco.

12. Amy works in a branch office in Arizona, but she wants to be transferred to the _____ of the company in LA.

13. At my office, there are many _____ . For example, my company is about 15% Hispanic.

14. I am going to _____ a job at another company.

15. I can't stand _____ . I spend half my day writing reports and reading letters.

YOUR TURN

1. In My Country . . .

In pairs or small groups, ask your classmates the questions below. When you finish, share the information with the class.

> 1. About how many hours a day do people work? How many hours a week?
> 2. Do office workers have to work overtime?
> 3. About how many holidays are there?
> 4. Are salaries high or low in business?
> 5. Do workers receive bonuses?
> 6. How much vacation do workers receive on average?
> 7. What other benefits do workers receive?
> 8. About what percentage of the work force are women or minorities?

2. Survey

Imagine the perfect job. Ask five members of your class for the information in the chart below. When you finish, discuss your answers with your classmates. What are the most popular types of jobs?

Name	Job Name	Job Description	Salary/Benefits
1.			
2.			
3.			
4.			
5.			

WORK TRANSCRIPT

Two business people, Mika and Arthur, are talking about their jobs over lunch.

Mika: So, how's your job, Arthur?

Arthur: Oh, Mika, it's the same. Same boss, same office, same people, everyday.

Mika: Sounds terrible!

Arthur: Yeah, and the paperwork gets me down. I hate filling out forms and writing reports.

Mika: Do you still hate your boss?

Arthur: Yeah, he's a real jerk. He hates it when anyone disagrees with him and I always disagree with him.

Mika: Why doesn't he fire you?

Arthur: He needs me too much. The guy is completely incompetent! (*pause*) I really want to quit!

Mika: I'm really sorry to hear that you're unhappy. Why don't you apply for other jobs? You have so much experience and an MBA from Harvard!

Arthur: Actually, I have applied for other jobs and I may have a job offer from Integrated Technologies.

Mika: Really?

Arthur: Yeah, they need someone in Personnel who knows a lot about computers.

Mika: That's great! I didn't know that they were hiring. They laid off a lot of people last year.

Arthur: Yeah, they did, but now they're growing again.

Mika: They have only average pay, but they have great benefits.

Arthur: Yeah, I know. Eleven holidays, four weeks paid vacation, and great medical coverage. They even have daycare.

Mika: They have a good reputation for their treatment of women and minorities. (*pause*) Of course that's not an advantage for you since you're a white male.

Arthur: They have a reputation for treating everyone fairly.

Mika: That's true.

Arthur: You know, I'm working about 10 hours of overtime per week!

Mika: I can't believe it! That's way too much.

Arthur: And the atmosphere is unbelievable in my office. Everyone is always trying to stab everyone else in the back! I hear all kinds of nasty stuff on the grapevine. (*pause*) So, how's your job?

Mika: It's wonderful. My boss is this really sweet, sensitive older man.

Arthur: You're really lucky!

Mika: He has a picture of his family on the desk and calls his 5-year-old once every day.

Arthur: My boss hates kids!

Mika: He insists that everyone take regular vacations because he's worried that we'll work too hard.

Arthur: I can't believe it!

Mika: I just got another promotion and a raise in pay.

Arthur: Stop! Don't tell me any more!

Mika: He gave me a $1000 bonus last week!

Arthur: That's unbelievable!

Mika: He said that I may be transferred from our branch office to corporate headquarters in New York because the company likes my work so much.

Arthur: Maybe I should apply at your company.

Mika: Well, you know they need someone in Personnel.

Arthur: Really? Who would I talk to?

Mika: Here, I'll write down the phone number and the name of the Director of Personnel.

Arthur: Thanks. I'll call this afternoon. (*pause*) Hey, it's really getting late. I'd better get out of here.

Mika: Me too. Say, it was really nice seeing you again. We'll have to get together again.

Arthur: Thanks for the encouragement. I'll see you.

CHAPTER NINETEEN

MOVIES AND TV

LISTENING

Look at the picture. What different kinds of movies are being shown?

Listen to the dialogue and fill in the blanks with T (true) or F (false). Listen again to check your answers.

Harry and Joan meet in a park.

_____ Joan has been seeing a lot of movies.

_____ She saw *Savage Love*.

_____ The acting in the movie was terrible.

_____ Mary Wells and Marvin Blake were in the movie.

_____ The movie was directed by Elisabeth Stone.

_____ Elisabeth Stone also directed *Maidstone Revisited*.

_____ *Maidstone Revisited* was shown in movie theaters.

_____ The lead actress was Jane Thatcher.

_____ *The Sampsons* is a TV comedy.

_____ *Star Travel* is a science fiction show.

_____ Joan has been watching a lot of dramas lately.

_____ Joan has cable TV.

_____ There are many different kinds of movies on cable.

_____ Harry recently saw a Spanish movie on TV.

_____ Joan thought *The 47 Samurai* was too violent.

_____ Harry and Joan may meet later in the week to watch movies on Harry's VCR.

FROM THE DIALOGUE

Study the vocabulary.

TYPES OF MOVIES AND TV PROGRAMS

action/adventure stories = thrilling and fast paced; sometimes violent
cartoons = movies or programs with no people, only drawings
classics = excellent movies from long ago
comedies/sitcoms = funny movies or programs
documentaries = showing true stories; no actors
dramas = serious movies or programs
foreign films = not from the USA
horror/monster = frightening movies or programs
murder mysteries/detective = movies or programs in which someone is killed
romances/love stories = about falling in love
science fiction = about the future or fantasy
westerns = about cowboys in the American West

OTHER TYPES OF TV PROGRAMS

game shows = people play a game to win money
news programs
soap operas = afternoon drama programs about people's lives
a series = a program that is on TV once a week
a mini-series = a program that lasts more than one night during one week (For example, Monday, Tuesday, and Wednesday nights)
shows = television programs

PARTS OF A MOVIE OR TV PROGRAM

the acting = the actions of the actors/actresses
commercials = a brief message which tries to sell a product
the costumes = the clothes
the director = the person who controls the making of the movie; he/she tells the actors, the writers, and the photographers what to do
the murderer = the person who kills someone
the producer = the company or person who pays the money for the movie to be made; the producer hires a director
the scenery = the background (mountains, houses, trees, gardens, etc.)
the script or screenplay = the words which the actors read
the victim = the person who is killed

RATING A MOVIE OR TV PROGRAM

terrific = very good
great = very good

terrible = very bad
lousy = very bad

TALKING ABOUT A MOVIE OR TV PROGRAM

What was it about?
Who else is in it?
It was **on TV.**

Marvin Blake **plays** the murder victim.
The movie **stars** Mary Wells.

TECHNOLOGY

network TV = the traditional television companies which send (broadcast) their programs through the air; these programs are free but have many commercials
cable TV = TV which comes from electrical wires connected to the TV rather than from the air. Cable has a larger number of programs with fewer commercials than network TV, but must be paid for.
VCR = a videocassette recorder; a machine to record programs or to play a videotape
videos = videotapes

CONVERSATION PRACTICE

1. Turn to page 188 and read the dialogue in pairs. Ask your teacher to explain any vocabulary or grammar you do not understand.

2. In pairs or small groups, complete each sentence with the correct word or phrase. Check your answers with the rest of your class.

director	game	action	screenplay	lousy

1. The acting in that movie was _____!
2. John Smith was the _____ of the movie.
3. I love _____ shows because of the money that's given away.
4. The _____ was written by Susan Bidley.
5. I usually don't like _____ movies because of the violence.

about	violent	on	cable	played

6. The movie was _____ TV last night.
7. Mark Komater _____ the murderer in that TV show.
8. The movie is _____ a young woman and her dog.
9. Do you have _____ TV?
10. That movie was too _____.

costumes	scenery	comedy	cartoon	documentary

11. I saw a _____ about poverty in the US.
12. He loved the _____ in that movie. It was shot in Scotland in the mountains.
13. I don't like _____. I prefer live actors.
14. She would like to see a _____ tonight because she feels like laughing.
15. The _____ in that movie were ugly.

| romances | dramas | detective | monster | soap opera |

16. _____ are really wonderful. I love seeing people in love.

17. Every afternoon, there is a _____ on that I really love. Right now, my favorite character is getting a divorce so that he can marry for the third time.

18. I didn't go see *Frankenstein, Godzilla,* or *King Kong* because I don't like _____ movies.

19. I am a very serious person, so I prefer _____ to comedies.

20. When I was a child, I wanted to be a police officer. I still love to go see _____ stories.

I don't like monster movies!

YOUR TURN

1. In pairs or small groups, fill in the blanks with the type of movie that is described. Then decide which movie you would prefer to see this Saturday night. Share your answer to the class.

1. _____ *King Kang*—A large gorilla destroys most of downtown Dallas.

2. _____ *Wild Grapes*—Two young people run away from home and get married despite their lack of money and parents' threats of suicide.

3. _____ *Lethal Force*—The police are baffled by thieves who blow up banks in downtown Cincinnati. A former detective who lost his job years ago seems to be their only chance.

4. _____ *Ciao Palermo*—A young boy leaves his hometown in Italy to seek his fortune in the big city of Rome. In Italian with English subtitles.

5. _____ *Campus Capers*—Young college pranksters drive their professors up the wall with their antics until the teaching staff calls in the army.

6. _____ *Krazy Rat*—A large rat and a cat fight each other constantly with various weapons. Their apartment is destroyed in the process, but they end up friends after all. Animated.

2. If . . .

1. If your life were made into a movie, what actor or actress would play you?
2. What other actors would be in the movie? Who would they play?
3. Who would direct the movie?
4. What kind of movie would it be? Briefly describe the plot.

3. Survey

Ask five members of your class for the information in the chart below. When you finish, compare your list with your classmates' lists. What are the most popular movies? What are the most popular TV shows?

Name	What is your favorite movie?	Why do you like it? Describe it in detail.	What is your favorite TV show?	Why do you like it? Describe it in detail.
1.				
2.				
3.				
4.				
5.				

MOVIES AND TV TRANSCRIPT

Harry and Joan meet in a park.

Harry: Hi, Joan.

Joan: Hey, Harry. How've you been?

Harry: Fine, thanks. What've you been up to lately?

Joan: Well, let me see. (*pause*) I guess that the only thing interesting that I've been doing is going to movies.

Harry: Really? What've you seen?

Joan: Saturday night I went to see *Savage Love.*

Harry: How was it?

Joan: Well, the acting was terrific!

Harry: Uh-huh.

Joan: The movie stars Mary Wells. She does a really good job as the murderer.

Harry: Who else is in it?

Joan: Well, Marvin Blake plays the murder victim. He's great!

Harry: Who was the director for that movie?

Joan: Uh, I think it was Elisabeth Stone, she also directed *Maidstone Revisited.* Do you remember it?

Harry: Not really. What was it about?

Joan: It was about a Catholic family in England.

Harry: Uh-huh.

Joan: They were really rich and had a lot of problems with alcoholism and love affairs.

Harry: I think that I did see it. It wasn't a movie; it was on TV.

Joan: Yeah, it was a mini-series during a whole week.

Harry: Sir Andrew Wyatt played the father, didn't he?

Joan: Yeah, and Jeremy Bartlett was the son's friend.

Harry: The scenery in that movie was incredible!

Joan: And the costumes were beautiful.

Harry: Wasn't the screenplay written by Jane Thatcher?

Joan: Yeah, it was. (*pause*) It's too bad that there are so few good shows on TV.

Harry: I watch *The Sampsons.*

Joan: I've never seen it; what's it about?

Harry: It's a cartoon family living in a typical American town.

Joan: Is it a comedy or drama?

Harry: It's a comedy. They make fun of everything American—like lawyers, greasy food, and violence on TV.

Joan: I thought that it was for kids!

Harry: No, it's for both kids and adults.

Joan: I watch *Star Travel.*

Harry: Is that the science fiction program?

Joan: Yeah, it's really nice because it's so optimistic about the future.

Harry: What do you mean?

Joan: I mean that in the 24th century people from Earth are more reasonable. There are fewer wars.

Harry: That sounds great!

Joan: I've also been watching a lot of documentaries recently.

Harry: I love documentaries!

Joan: Last night there was a program about political problems in South America, Africa, and Asia.

Harry: That sounds really interesting.

Joan: Yeah, it was. The BBC was the producer.

Harry: (*pause*) Do you have cable TV?

Joan: No, do you?

Harry: Yeah. It's expensive, but there are so many movies on cable that I stay home instead of spending a lot at a movie theater.

Joan: What kind of movies do they show?

Harry: Classic movies, foreign films , detective movies, romances, adventure stories, documentaries —all kinds of movies, even monster movies.

Joan: I suppose I'll have to get cable.

Harry: It's worth it. Network TV has too many commercials and I get tired of game shows and soap operas. (*pause*) By the way, I saw an old Matsumoto movie from the '50s last night!

Joan: Which one was it?

Harry: The *47 Samurai.*

Joan: I thought that movie was terrible!

Harry: Why?

Joan: It was too violent and the acting was lousy!

Harry: It was rather violent.

Joan: That's why I don't like westerns.

Harry: I don't really like them either.

Joan: (*pause*) Well, I'm really glad that I ran into you today.

Harry: Why don't you come over some evening and we'll watch some movies.

Joan: That sounds great! Do you have a VCR?

Harry: Yeah, we can rent a couple of videos and eat popcorn.

Joan: That sounds wonderful.

Harry: Call me sometime this week.

Joan: I'll do that. See you next week!

Harry: Bye.

CHAPTER TWENTY

TELEPHONE LANGUAGE

LISTENING

Do you like to talk on the telephone? Who do you like to talk to? What do you talk about?

Listen to each dialogue and fill in the blanks with T (true) or F (false). Listen again to check your answers.

1. *Sergei calls Anna to invite her to a concert.*

_____ Sergei wants to speak to Sonya.

_____ Sonya is studying for her final exams.

_____ Sergei has two tickets to a classical music concert.

_____ The concert is at 8:00.

_____ Anna is at her brother's house.

_____ Sonya does not like Beethoven.

_____ Sonya will pay for dinner if Sergei takes her to the concert.

_____ Sonya will pick up Sergei.

2. *John calls his classmate, Jackie.*

_____ John is in Jackie's history class.

_____ The man tells John that Jackie is not there.

_____ John says he'll call back later.

_____ The man says that it's O.K. for John to call back later.

3. *Margarite calls about a job.*

_____ Margarite calls Thornton Computers to apply for a job as a manager.

_____ The Director's name is Helen.

_____ The position is only temporary.

_____ Margarite has two years experience as a secretary/receptionist.

_____ Margarite has a BA in accounting.

_____ Margarite and the director will meet the next day at 10:00.

_____ Margarite doesn't know where the office building is.

FROM THE DIALOGUES

Study the vocabulary.

IDENTIFYING YOURSELF

Good afternoon, Thornton Computers.
Hello. My name is Margarite Powers.
Hello. This is Susan.
This is Sonya.
Hi. This is Sergei.
I'm John. **I'm** in her Chemistry class.

ASKING FOR A NAME

May I say who's calling?

STATING YOUR PURPOSE FOR CALLING

This is especially important for business calls.

I'm calling about the secretary position advertised in the newspaper.

ASKING FOR A MESSAGE

Would you like me to give her a message?
Can I take a message?

FINDING THE RIGHT PERSON

I'll check and see if Anna's **here.**
I'll get her.
I'll see if I can find her.
I'll transfer you to the Director of Personnel.

GIVING A MESSAGE

Tell her (that) I have two tickets for the Berlin Philharmonic tomorrow night at Carnegie Hall at 8:00.
No, I'll just call back later.
I'll try back tomorrow.

THE PERSON IS NOT THERE

I'm sorry, but she's not here.
I'm sorry, but she must have stepped out.
I'm sorry, but you must have the wrong number.

PLEASE WAIT

Just a second.
Just a minute.

IDIOMS

I know what you mean. = I understand.
I'll tell you what. = I am making a proposal.
You've got a deal. = I agree to your conditions.

CONVERSATION PRACTICE

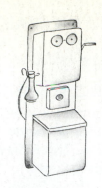

1. *Go to page 197 and read the dialogues in pairs. In the final dialogue, one person should read both the person who answers the phone and the director. Ask your teacher to explain any vocabulary or grammar you do not understand.*

2. *Match the sentences in Column One with the sentences in Column Two. The first one is done for you.*

Column One

_____h____ May I say who's calling

_____ Good afternoon, IBJ Chemicals.

_____ Why don't you come over tomorrow afternoon?

_____ Hello.

_____ Hello. Is Betty there?

_____ May I speak to Peter?

_____ Would you like me to give him a message?

_____ I'll check and see if he's here.

_____ I'll tell you what. You lend me $50 and I'll take you out to dinner at a nice restaurant.

_____ I'm calling about the manager position advertised in the paper.

_____ Hello, is Suzie there?

_____ I've got tests coming up, so I'm working really hard.

_____ I'm sorry, but she must have stepped out.

_____ I'd like to speak to Ms. Murphy in Personnel.

Column Two

a. Hello. This is Harry. May I speak to Joan.

b. I'm sorry, but he's not here.

c. I know what you mean.

d. Yes, please. Tell him that Andre called.

e. Thanks. I appreciate it.

f. You've got a deal!

g. This is Suzie.

h. I'm William Kent.

i. Oh, that's too bad. I was hoping to talk to her.

j. Hello. May I speak to your office manager?

k. I'm sorry, but that position has already been filled.

l. Hold on. I'll transfer you.

m. Well, actually, I already have an appointment then. How about tomorrow morning?

n. Betty? I'm sorry, but you must have the wrong number.

3. Put the conversations in the correct order by numbering the sentences. The first one is done for you.

1. _____ Oh, hi Jenny. How're you doing?

   _____ He's in the shower. Can you call back in about 20 minutes?

   _____ Yes, I do.

   _____ Hello.

   __1__ Yes?

   _____ Good night.

   _____ Sure, no problem. Well, it was nice talking to you. Maybe I'll see you this weekend.

   _____ Hello. This is Jenny.

   _____ I'm glad to hear that. Do you want to speak to Mac?

   _____ Yeah, drop over anytime.

   _____ Just a second. I'll get him. (*pause*) Jenny?

   _____ Fine thanks. I'm really busy, but business is good.

2. _____ I'd love to. Say hello to your family for me.

   _____ Just fine thanks. Business is a bit slow, but we're O.K.

   _____ Oh, hi Mark. This is Carol.

   _____ I will. Bye.

   _____ Well, that's too bad about business, but it'll pick up later in the year. How's little Henry?

   __1__ Good morning. Jackson Building Supplies.

   _____ Little Henry is now 16 years old and is 6' 2" tall.

   _____ O.K., it was really nice talking to you again. You'll have to drop by some time.

   _____ It is amazing, isn't it. (*pause*) Did you need to make an order?

   _____ Hello. This is Mark over at City Hall.

   _____ I can't believe it. Where did the time go?

   _____ An order? Oh, yeah, I wanted to get some . . . let me see . . . what was it? (*pause*) Oh, I'd better ask George what it was. I'll call you back.

   _____ Carol! It's good to hear your voice. How've you been?

YOUR TURN

1. Roleplays

In pairs, choose a role and follow the instructions for the telephone call. When you finish your call, switch roles and do the exercise again. Sit in your chair or desk with your back to your partner while doing the roleplay.

> **Key Phrases**
> Hello, this is _____ .
> May I speak to _____ ?
> I'm sorry, but he/she's not here right now. May I take a message?
> Please tell him/her that _____ called to tell him/her
>   that _____ .
> I was wondering if you'd like to _____ .

Roleplay 1:

Student A: You have to call your friend John to find out if he is going to Sarah's party Saturday night. If he isn't at home, leave a message with his roommate. You know John's roommate fairly well. You both love soccer (football).

Student B: You are home alone. Your roommate John is shopping at the mall. He'll be back in the evening. You love soccer and often go to matches with friends.

Roleplay 2:

Student A: You are the receptionist at Beacon Corporation. Your boss, Ms. Albertson, is out of the office. It is now afternoon.

Student B: You are a manager at the Walton Corporation. You need to know when Beacon Corporation's new computer accounting software will be on the market. Call Ms. Betty Albertson, a manager at Beacon Corporation, to find out. If she is not there, leave a message.

Roleplay 3:

Student A: You are calling your friend Karl to see if he would like to go see a movie tonight. The movie is *Attack of the 50-Foot Frogs*. The special effects in this movie are supposed to be incredible. The movie starts at 8:00. It costs $7.00. Karl just broke up with his girlfriend so you are worried that he is depressed.

Student B: Your name is Karl. You are really bored. It's Saturday and you have no plans for tonight because you and your girlfriend just broke up. You are a little depressed. You would like to get back together with your girlfriend.

2. If . . .

If you could make a telephone call to anyone in the world, living or dead, who would it be? What would you say? Make some notes and then act out the telephone call with a partner.

TELEPHONE LANGUAGE TRANSCRIPT

1. Sergei calls Anna to invite her to a concert
   (the phone rings)

Sonya: Hello.

Sergei: Hi. This is Sergei. May I speak to Anna?

Sonya: Oh, hi Sergei. This is Sonya.

Sergei: Hi, Sonya. How's it going?

Sonya: Fine, but finals are coming up, so I'm studying like crazy.

Sergei: Yeah, I know what you mean.

Sonya: Well, it was nice talking to you. I'll check and see if Anna's still here.

Sergei: Thanks. *(pause)*

Sonya: I'm sorry, but she's not here. Would you like me to give her a message?

Sergei: Yes. I'd appreciate that. Tell her that I have two tickets for the Berlin Philharmonic tomorrow night at Carnegie Hall at 8:00. They're playing Beethoven and Mozart.

Sonya: Oh, well . . . I know that she'd love to go with you, but I don't think that she's going to be back tomorrow.

Sergei: Really?

Sonya: Yeah, she went to her parents' house for the weekend.

Sergei: Well, I don't know what to do. My brother gave me these two tickets and I hate to waste the other one.

Sonya: Well, actually, I love Beethoven and Mozart!

Sergei: Really? Well, maybe this will work out after all.

Sonya: I'll tell you what. You take me to the symphony and I'll buy you dinner at that new Chinese Restaurant downtown.

Sergei: You've got a deal. I'll pick you up at 6:00.

Sonya: Great. I'll see you at six. I really appreciate this.

Sergei: I'm looking forward to seeing you again.

Sonya: Bye!

2. John calls his classmate, Jackie.
   (the phone rings)

Man: Hello.

John: Hello. Is Jackie there?

Man: Sure, just a second. I'll get her. May I say who's calling?

John: I'm John. I'm in her Chemistry class.

Man: O.K., just a minute. I'll see if I can find her. *(pause)* I'm sorry, but she must have stepped out. Can I take a message?

John: No, I'll just call back later.

Man: Well, we usually go to sleep in about an hour.

John: Sleep? Oh, well, I'll, uh, try back tomorrow. I mean that, well, tell her it wasn't that important.

Man: O.K. I'll give her the message.

John: Thanks.

3. Margarite calls about a job.
   (the phone rings)

Jane: Good afternoon, Thornton Computers.

Margarite: Um . . . I'm calling about the secretary position advertised in the newspaper.

Jane: Just a minute. I'll transfer you to the Director of Personnel. She's doing the hiring.

Margarite: O.K. *(pause)*

Susan: Hello. This is Susan.

Margarite: Hello. My name is Margarite Powers and I'm calling about the secretary position you advertised in the newspaper.

Susan: Yes, we need someone right away on a temporary basis.

Margarite: I'm available immediately.

Susan: What experience do you have?

Margarite: Well, I worked for Payrolls Are Us, Incorporated for two years in their headquarters. I was a secretary/receptionist. I also have an Associates Degree in accounting and I am studying nights for my BA.

Susan: Well, that sounds fine. Why don't you come over sometime tomorrow for an interview?

Margarite: That sounds good to me.

Susan: How about 10:00? I'm free then.

Margarite: That would be good for me too. I'll bring my resume. (*pause*) Uh, I know your building, but what's your office number?

Susan: 436.

Margarite: 436.

Susan: O.K. I'll see you tomorrow.

Margarite: Yes. I'll see you at 10:00.

Susan: Bye.

REVIEW

CHAPTERS 11-20

1. Scrambled Conversation

Put the conversation in the correct order by numbering the sentences. The first one is done for you

_____ That's terrible.

_____ I heard that it's really good.

_____ Well, a C's not too bad. (*pause*) How're you and John doing?

_____ You're right. Let's go!

_____ O.K. I guess, but I think I just flunked a major chemistry test.

_____ I'd love to, but I'm really too depressed.

_____ Really, that's a surprise!

_____ Come on. It'll do you good to get out and stop thinking about John.

_____ He's always been kind of a jerk.

_____ Yeah.

___1___ Hi Joe. How've you been?

_____ Fine thanks, Mary. How's school?

_____ Terrible, we broke up.

_____ Well, I've got to get going. I'm going to see the new Rene Auberjine movie down at the Castro Theater.

_____ It'll be all right. I'm doing really well in everything else and I'll still be able to pull out a C in chemistry.

_____ Me too. Why don't you come with me?

_____ It shouldn't be a surprise. He's been going out with two other girls.

2. Interview

In pairs, interview a partner using the questions below. Report the answers to the class. Your teacher will tell you which questions to answer or not.

1. What is your best subject in school? Why?
2. What kind of person are you? Describe yourself in detail.
3. What makes you sad? What makes you happy? Give detailed reasons why.
4. Briefly tell about your life so far. Where were you born? Where have you lived? Where have you traveled? Give details.
5. Have you ever had a job? If so, describe it in detail (For example: hours, benefits, responsibilities).
6. Describe a movie that you have seen lately. Tell your partner about it. Did you like it? Why or why not?
7. What was your most exciting experience? Give details.

3. Vocabulary

Complete each sentence with the correct word or words

goofing off	cram	major	flunk	Ph.D.

1. I haven't studied for my history test. I'll have to _____ for it tonight.
2. If I _____ this test, I'll be in big trouble!
3. Mary has an MA in physics and a _____ in biology.
4. John's not a serious student. He's always _____.
5. My _____ in college was business.

yuck	ouch	oops	O.K.	uh-oh

1. _____ , I dropped a glass of milk on the carpet.
2. _____ , this tastes terrible!
3. _____ , I forgot to lock the car door.
4. Hey Mom. Is it _____ if I go to the movie with my friends?
5. _____ , I cut my hand with a knife.

sweetheart	brain	jock	redneck	slob

1. She's a real _____ . She never cleans up her room.
2. John's such a _____ ! He studies all day on Saturday and Sunday.
3. Mary's such a _____ . She's always playing some sport.
4. Harry is very conservative. He drives a pick-up truck. He's a real _____ .
5. Harry's a real _____ . He always helps me when I have a problem.

sick and tired of	crazy about	homesick
upsets		get along with

1. I'm _____ chocolate ice cream. I eat it every day.
2. I'm _____ my brother complaining.
3. I get _____ when I travel.
4. I _____ John because he's so friendly.
5. Jerry _____ me when he talks about my bad grammar.

happened	widow	divorce	affair	married

1. I heard that Amy had a love _____ with Joe.
2. Mary became a _____ in 1979 when her husband Harry died.
3. Kim got a _____ four months ago. She wants to marry again.
4. What _____ after that?
5. Helen and Mark got _____ last spring. The wedding was beautiful.

hired	holiday	promotion	raise	bonus

1. Martin Luther King's birthday is a _____ in most states.
2. Rosemary was given a big _____ in salary by her boss.
3. Sam was _____ last year. As a new employee, his salary is rather low.
4. Because of her excellent performance, Sally was given a large year-end

   _____ .
5. Joe got a _____ from Supervisor to Assistant Manager last month.

transferred	applied	quit	incompetent	benefits

1. Patsy _____ her job because of problems with her boss.
2. Harry was _____ from Atlanta to New York.
3. Jane _____ for a job at the new factory.
4. My boss is really _____ . He can't do anything right.
5. At my company, _____ include medical coverage and vacation pay.

directed	cartoons	played	dramas	documentary

1. I've always loved _____ more than
   films with real people.
2. I don't like comedies . I prefer _____ .
3. Last night I saw a _____ about
   French cooking.
4. Who _____ that film?
5. In the movie, Harold Johnson, a new actor,
   _____ the killer.

by the way	later	actually	nevermind	tell him

1. _____ I called to ask if he wants to go to a movie tonight.
2. _____ , I'll do the vacuuming myself!
3. _____ , where were you last night?
4. No, I'll just call back_____ .
5. _____ , I love classical music. I'm just crazy about Mozart.

6. Mock Cocktail Party

You are going to a party in your classroom. Before the party, you are going to create a new identity for yourself. To do this, you must answer the questions below the night before the party. You must be a new person, but not a famous person, from the past or present.

1. What is your new name? What sex are you (*male* or *female*)?
2. What country are you from?
3. What is your occupation?
4. What are your hobbies?
5. What is your marital status (*married, single, divorced, widowed*)?
6. Do you have any children?
7. How old are you?
8. What type of personality (*happy, sad, talkative, curious, shy, boring, exciting, dynamic, lazy, lively*) and character (*workaholic, sweetheart, nerd*) are you?
9. Where have you traveled?
10. What is the most interesting thing that has ever happened to you?
11. What is the most terrible thing that has ever happened to you?
12. What are your accomplishments? (Have you ever written a book, climbed a mountain, captured a thief, played lead guitar in a heavy metal rock band, etc.?)

Cocktail Party Guidelines

You do not know any of the other people at the party because they also have new identities. You will have to introduce yourself to everyone and tell them about yourself. Then, you will have to converse about a variety of subjects (such as the weather, music, sports). You may bring some cups and something non-alcoholic to drink. Your teacher will be the bartender.

SOME HELPFUL HINTS

1. Arrive a little bit late (1–2 minutes).
2. Greet the host (your teacher).
3. Talk to *everyone* during the party.
4. Introduce yourself to people you do not know. (*How do you do? I'm _____ .*)
5. Say good-bye to the host before leaving.
6. Compliment the host. (*It was a wonderful party! I had a great time!*)

1. If you don't understand something, ask a question. (*Could you repeat that?*)

2. If you do understand, say something to show that you understand.
   (*Uh-huh, Really?, How nice!*)

3. If you need time to think, use an appropriate expression. (*Hmmm, Let me think, Well . . .*)

4. Avoid silence. (5 seconds is too much)

5. Give complete responses to questions, not only *yes* or *no*.

6. Ask open questions (*How did you like _____? What's _____ like?*).

APPENDIX

CARD SHEET

Chapter 8: Explanations, Page 85, Your Turn, Exercise 2, Explain It To Me, Variation 1.
Use the cards below or make your own.

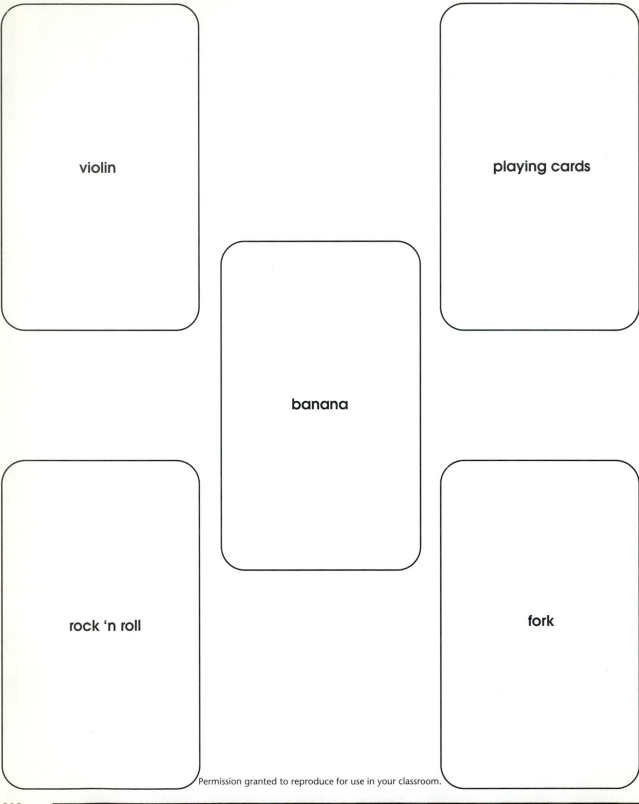

violin

playing cards

banana

rock 'n roll

fork

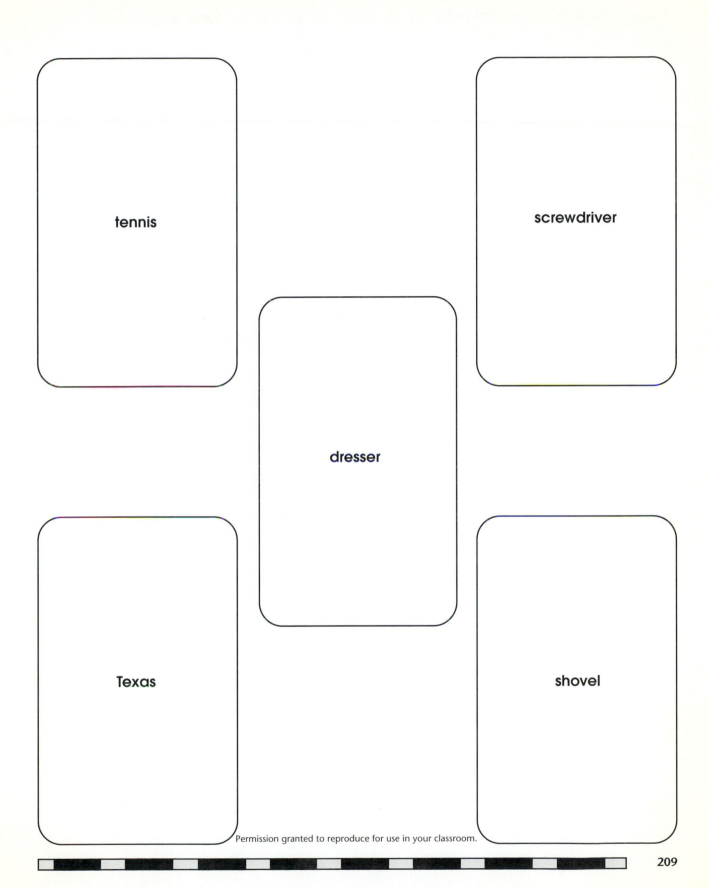

tennis

screwdriver

dresser

Texas

shovel

TAPESCRIPT

Chapter 10: Reduced Forms, Page 98

DICTATION	NORMAL WRITTEN FORM
1. **Wha-dja** do this weekend?	1. What did you do this weekend?
2. I'm **gonna** go **da** the beach.	2. I'm going to the beach.
3. What's **yer** name?	3. What's your name?
4. I've **gotta** go.	4. I've got to go.
5. I **wanna** go home.	5. I want to go home.
6. I **hafta** study harder.	6. I have to study harder.
7. **Ya awda** get a job.	7. You ought to get a job.
8. Where **dya** go **da** school?	8. Where do you go to school?
9. Where **dja** go **da** school?	9. Where did you go to school?
10. He **must-uv** forgotten.	10. He must have forgotten.
11. **Wha-duv-ya** been **doin'**?	11. What have you been doing?
12. How **er ya doin'**?	12. How are you doing?
13. **Wha-der-ya gonna** do tomorrow?	13. What are you going to do tomorrow?
14. **Dya wanna** go **da** the beach?	14. Do you want to go to the beach?
15. I **dunno** his name.	15. I don't know his name.
16. I've been **thinkin'** **'bout** my future.	16. I've been thinking about my future.
17. Are **ya** O.K.?	17. Are you O.K.?
18. **Wha-dya wanna** do?	18. What do you want to do?
19. She **hasta** stay home tonight.	19. She has to stay home tonight.
20. **Ya** been **'ere** long?	20. Have you been here long?

TAPESCRIPT

Review of Chapters 1–10, Page 109 Exercise 6, Reduced Forms

DICTATION	NORMAL WRITTEN FORM
1. **Wha-der-ya gonna** do this weekend?	1. What are you going to do this weekend?
2. **Dya wanna** go **swimmin'**?	2. Do you want to go swimming?
3. He's **gotta** get up early.	3. He's got to get up early.
4. You guys **awda** be careful.	4. You guys ought to be careful.
5. I **hafta** do some homework.	5. I have to do some homework.
6. Have **ya** been **'ere** long?	6. Have you been here long?
7. I **dunno** anything **'bout** it.	7. I don't know anything about it.
8. **Don-chya** think that'll be difficult?	8. Don't you think that'll be difficult?
9. I **wanna** get **awda** here.	9. I want to get out of here.
10. How're **ya gonna** do it?	10. How are you going to do it?

CARD SHEET

Chapter 14: Conversational Expressions, Page 141, Your Turn, Exercise 1, Chit-Chat.
Use the cards below or make your own.

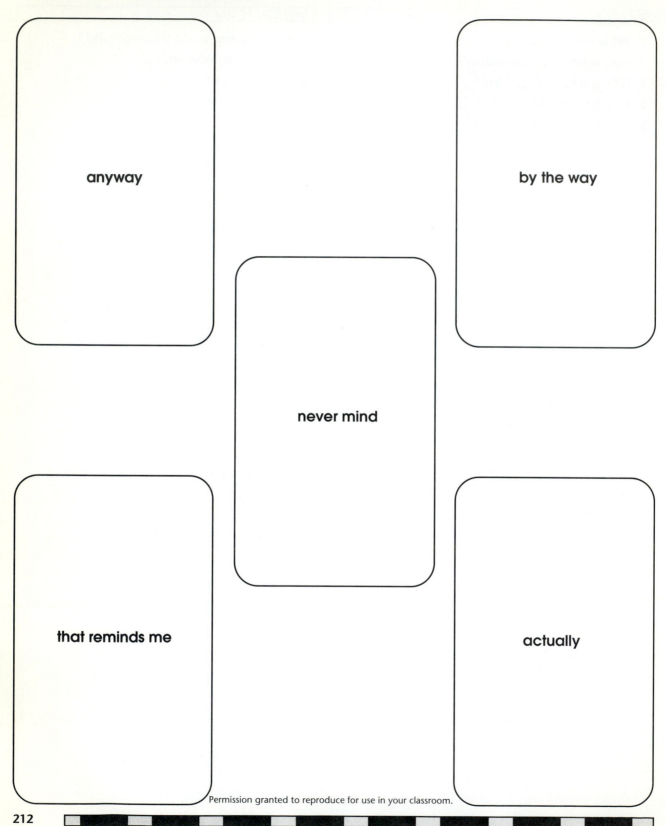

anyway

by the way

never mind

that reminds me

actually

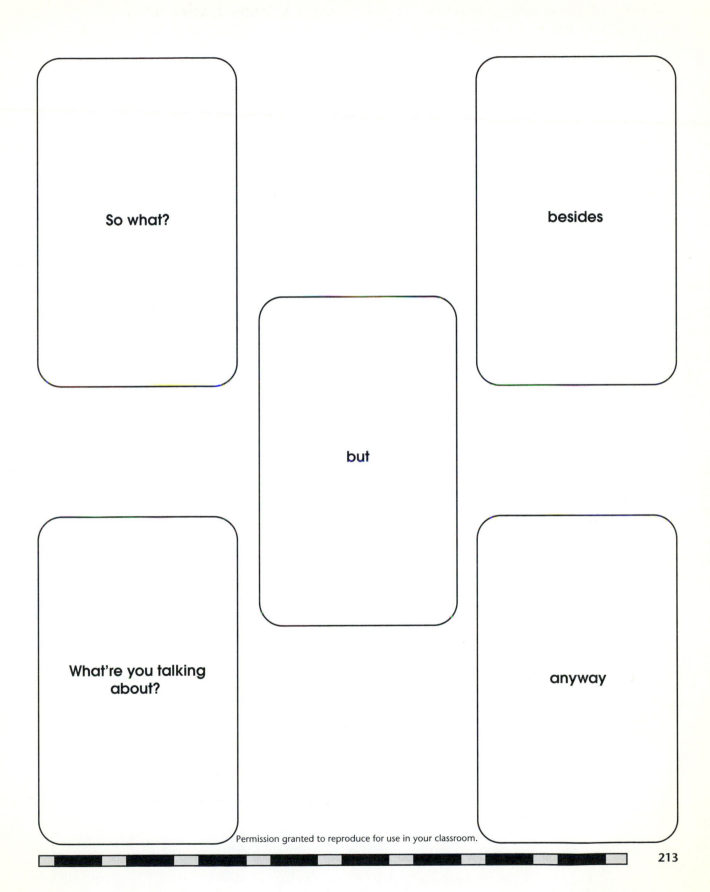

So what?

besides

but

What're you talking about?

anyway

by the way

never mind

that reminds me

actually

So what?

besides

What're you talking about?

but

FOLLOW-UP DISCUSSIONS

Ask students what topics in their culture are considered inappropriate to discuss with people they do not know well. Have them compare these topics to topics that may be considered inappropriate in this situation in U. S. culture.

Ask if students have expressions like *T. G. I. F.* (*Thank God It's Friday*), *Blue Monday*, and Hump Day (i.e. Wednesday) in their native language.

Natural disasters, such as a *tornado, hurricane, earthquake, tidal wave, drought, flood,* or *heat wave*, provide an easy bridge to discussion. Students can talk about the various disasters that have struck their countries or potentially could strike their countries. This discussion can even lead to environmental topics: the Greenhouse effect, a new ice age, destruction of the ozone, oil spills, acid rain. Let the students lead the discussion to what interests them

1. If you have students who are interested in political issues, ask about cultural imperialism. How do they feel about American jazz, pop, and rock and roll dominating world music and, in many cases, driving native forms underground? The expansion of MTV to South America and other areas is a rather controversial topic for some students. How do yours feel about it?
2. Does the content of some modern music influence the listeners? If so, to what extent? Does rap cause violence?
3. Have students describe, or even bring in samples, of music from their country or region, If there is a student who has a folk instrument, ask him/her to bring it in and play. A *kora* from North Africa or a *koto* from Japan really adds zest to a class.

Have the students explain even more objects and customs indigenous to their countries or regions.

1. If your students are politically minded, a discussion of the worldwide social, ethical, and nutritional implications of meat eating might bring about a rousing discussion. Should first world countries be allowing their cattle to eat so much grain when so many people are starving in the third world? Is overgrazing going to turn much of the world into a desert?
2. Do humans have the right to kill and eat other species? How do we know that lobsters feel no pain when they are being boiled?
3. Does red wine really help prevent heart disease when drunk in small quantities? How do the French get away with eating all that fatty food without having a tremendous problem with heart disease? Some useful additional vocabulary includes: *cholesterol, saturated fats, vitamins, minerals, veins and arteries, hardening of the arteries, heart disease, heart attack, triple by-pass*

Use the following jokes as a wrap up to the chapter. Write them on the board.

A: My aunt went to an island in the Caribbean.

B: Jamaica?

A: No, she wanted to go.

A: My uncle lives in a city in Alaska?

B: Nome?

A: Of course I know 'im. He's my uncle. Aren't you listening?

Follow-up vocabulary: words for plural you—*y'all, you all, youse;* and *howdy* from *How do you do?*

CHAPTER 11: SCHOOL

The United States is generally cited as the country with the greatest emphasis on post-high school education. The U.S. has a startlingly wide variety of junior colleges, vo-tech institutes, adult education schools, small private certificate programs, colleges with ties to a particular church (Southern Methodist, Notre Dame), traditionally Black colleges (Bethune-Cookman in Florida), traditionally Jewish universities (Yeshiva), women's colleges, and large private and public universities. Schools in the U.S. often emphasize general studies longer than programs in other countries. Further, it is much easier to get into a college in the U.S. than in most other countries, and it is easier to fail than in some other countries, such as France and Japan. In many colleges in the U.S. the attrition rate between acceptance as a freshman and graduation is over 50%. Finally, the university in the U.S. is often seen as a separate community within a community. Campuses have stores, movie theaters, banks, swimming pools, and parks. They are mini-cities. This is not true in many countries.

1. Have students compare their educational systems to the system in the U.S., Canada, Britain, New Zealand, or other English-speaking countries. The U.S. in particular may have a radically different underlying philosophy from what students are used to.

2. What do the students think are the strengths and weaknesses of the U.S. system? Would a more focused course of studies beginning in high school be better for the people and the country?

3. Should so many people be given the opportunity for higher education or should it be restricted to the intellectual elite?

4. Should the continued existence of colleges for special groups be allowed or encouraged? (e.g. Black colleges) Are quotas in some cases unjust? At the University of California at Berkeley, the student body is now dominated by Asians. Each year, some Asians are denied entry so that other ethnic groups can enter. This is because of the university's commitment to a diverse student body.

5. In the United States, there has been the traditional emphasis on European culture (often termed the history of the *D.W.M.—Dead White Man*). Ideas from western civilization dominate classes in history and philosophy. Is this "Euro-centrism" unfair to African-Americans, Latinos, and Asian-Americans? What does this issue say about the nature of the U.S.? Is it a European country?

6. Have students tour a U.S. college campus.

CHAPTER 13: PEOPLE

Students who are studying American English to go to the U.S. need to know "politically correct" or "P. C." words. Words for ethnic and sexual groups are very important, such as *person of color, gay and lesbian, Hispanic, feminist, Euro-Americans,* and *Native Americans.* There is also a whole new vocabulary for what used to be called the handicapped. Now they are *physically challenged* or *differently abled.* It should be explained to students that the objective of P.C. words is to give equal treatment to people who are different or in the minority. Stereotypes must be avoided.

1. Students can discuss the implications of Affirmative Action and the Americans with Disabilities Act (ADA) for people who do business in the U.S.
2. Some foreign students have gotten into trouble in the U.S. for doing things that were perceived as insensitive on their part. What behaviors that are acceptable in their cultures could be considered inappropriate in U.S. culture?
3. How do the students feel about gay rights, women's rights, or any of the other rights movements?

Further vocabulary includes: *stud, wannabe, couch potato, dink, wimp, yuppie, buppie,* and *punk.*

CHAPTER 15: FEELINGS

1. In some countries, feelings are discussed and openly expressed; in others, feelings are hidden or covered up. On a scale from 1–10, with 1 being total frankness and 10 being a lack of emotional expression, what numbers do the students feel best represent their countries? What are the advantages and disadvantages of the different positions on the expression of feelings?
2. Ask Europeans about perceived differences between Southern Europe and Northern Europe. Ask about the perceived differences between North and South America. Ask the Japanese students to explain what *tatemae* and *honne* mean.

CHAPTER 16: STORYTELLING

Ask students to continue to tell stories about their experiences. At the beginning of the school week and after vacations, students should be asked for one detailed anecdote about their experiences.

CHAPTER 17: LIFE

1. Discuss the English kinship system and have the students compare it to the system in their native culture. Do they have *step- foster- adopted-* or *half-sisters* and *brothers*? Do they have *second cousins (kissing cousins), biological mothers, surrogate mothers*?
2. How are names formed in the different cultures? Some students may have only one name (e.g. some Indonesians). Americans usually have three names. Do any students have both their mother's and father's names? Do the names have meanings, such as *Yamaguchi* meaning *mouth of the mountain*? What does each student's name mean?
3. What is a good life? What should people do with their lives? What is the most useful or noblest occupation? How can we judge a life? Have students discuss the quotation by Herodotus who said, "We cannot evaluate a life until it is over."

CHAPTER 18: WORK

Ask the students where they want to be in 20 years. What kind of job do they want to have (be realistic)? What kind of income? What kind of family? What kind of housing? Next, ask them where they will have to be in 10 years to be on track for their 20-year goal. Where must they be in 5 years? What must they do this year to begin the trek to their 20-year goal? Vocational counselors use this exercise to force students to think of the future as a logical conclusion to what they are doing today. Feel free to point out illogical statements or unrealistic expectations. To succeed in the competitive world, students need to be firmly grounded. If they are late for class everyday and turn in only half of their homework, chances are they will not be corporate executives 20 years from now.

CHAPTER 19: MOVIES AND TV

Give students several short movie reviews to read. Include a variety of styles (e.g. Vincent Canby of the *New York Times* and Joe Bob Briggs). Students should then be shown a movie and asked to review it in groups. A written review can be the final product. Scenes from the television show "At the Movies," "Sneak Previews," or another film review program would expose the students to rapid-fire vocabulary and idioms for talking about movies, such as "Dog of the Week".

CHAPTER 20: TELEPHONE LANGUAGE

Have the students each call you at home **once** (depending on how much work you can stand at home). In the U.S., 1–800 numbers provide incredible opportunities for free information gathering. Watch TV commercials and write them all down. 1-900 numbers can work also, but can become rather expensive. Local calls to movie theaters to find out starting times work well for listening comprehension practice, as does calling for restaurant hours. Try to spread these calls over many businesses as a plague of limited-English-proficiency phone calls to one business might not be appreciated as much as one would assume.

ANSWER KEY

CHAPTER ONE

Listening

1. At a party

   T, F ,F ,T, F, F, T, F, T

2. Making a plane reservation

   F, T, F ,F, T, F, F

Conversation Practice

2. In pairs . . .

   A variety of answers are acceptable.

3. In pairs . . .

   1. On Thursday?
   2. 6009?
   3. In 1985?
   4. The Regency Hotel?
   5. New Hampshire?

4. Corrections

   Some variation in answers is inevitable here. Answers given are suggestions.

   1. No, actually I said Austria.
   2. No, that's not quite right. It's four weeks, not four months.
   3. That's not quite right. It's Jose, not Juan.
   4. No, I'm sorry, but I think that you've made a mistake. She's arriving on the 30th. That's three-zero.

5. WH-questions

   1. What did you see?
   2. When are you going home?
   3. Where are you going?
   4. What are you going to buy?
   5. Who is from Senegal?
   6. Where is the weather beautiful?
   7. When is he flying to Vancouver?

6. Confirming numbers

   1. Did you say one-three or three zero?
   2. Is that one-five?
   3. Did you say four-zero St.?
   4. Is that one-eight or eight-zero?

7. Scrambled Conversation

   12, 3, 4, 6, 10, 8, 9, 13, 1, 11, 14, 2, 5, 7

CHAPTER TWO

Listening

1. Steve goes into his Boss' office.

   T, T

2. At work

   T, F

3. Two high school students meet.

   T, F,

4. Tomonori and Jae meet at a museum.

   T, F

5. Three people meet at a restaurant.

   F, T

6. At a supermarket

   F, T, T

7. Two couples meet at a dance.

   F, T, T, F

Conversation Practice

2. Best Answer

   1. b
   2. d

3. Matching

   g, d, f, c, a, b, e

4. Write Openers

   1. How's Kumiko?
      I hope Kumiko's feeling better.
      Is Kumiko OK?

   2. What a beautiful necklace!
      I love your necklace!|
      That's a really nice necklace!

   3. Did you see the game last night?
      Did you hear about the Dodgers game?
      How about those Dodgers?

   4. Have you gone to the new symphony yet?
      What do you think about the new symphony?
      I went to the symphony last night.

5. How was Japan?
   Tell me about your trip to Japan.
   I heard that you just got back from
   Japan.

5. Scrambled Conversations

   1. 4, 1, 5, 2, 3, 6
   2. 3, 6, 1, 5, 4, 2
   3. 6, 2, 4, 3, 5, 1
   4. 2, 1, 4, 6, 3, 5

CHAPTER THREE

Listening

1. Two students meet after summer vacation.

   T, F, T, T, F, F, T, F

2. A boy is describing his day to his father.

   T, F, T, T, T, F, F

Conversation Practice

2. Listener Expressions

   Various answers are appropriate. Sentences given are only examples.

   1. That's great!
   2. That's too bad!
   3. I'm sorry to hear that!
   4. That must have been interesting!
   5. Uh-huh.
   6. I'm sorry to hear that.
   7. I'm glad to hear that!
   8. Great!

3. Open Questions.

   2, 4, 5, 6, 7, 8, and 10 are open questions.

4. Write one description and one opinion question and replies.

   Various answers are possible. Sentences given are just examples.

   1. Q: How was the concert?
      A: It was boring.
      Q: What was the concert like?
      A: It was really crowded.

2. Q: What did you think of India?
   A: It was wonderful!
   Q: Could you tell me about India?
   A: Well, it was hot, but exotic and the food was *incredible!*

3. Q: Why did you go there?
   A: Because we read about it in the newspaper.

   Q: What was the restaurant like?
   A: It was dirty and the food was awful.

7. Scrambled Conversations

   7, 14, 8, 13, 2, 5, 12, 9, 3, 10, 1, 11, 6, 4

CHAPTER FOUR

Listening

1. Amy has to go home to study.

   F, F ,F, T

2. Pon and Fyodor are talking. Pon has to go home.

   T, F, T

3. Mary and Susan are talking. Mary is going home after a visit to the city.

   T, T, F

Conversation Practice

2. P, P, X, M, W, X, C, P, M, P, X

4. Scrambled Conversation

   3, 7, 4, 2, 8, 6, 1, 5

REVIEW OF CHAPTERS 1–4

1. June runs into Lee in a supermarket.

   6, 1, 5, 7, 8, 3, 4, 9, 2

2. May and Jonathan meet in their university library.

   4, 6, 2, 9, 7, 3, 1, 8, 5

Matching

   d, c, i, e, a, j, h, f, b, g

CONVERSATION MAZE ONE

   Answers are in the maze.

CHAPTER FIVE

Listening

1. Patsy and Mark meet on Monday morning.

    F, T, F

2. David and Ken meet on Friday afternoon.

    T, T, F, F

Conversation Practice

3. Scrambled sentences.

    3, 11, 6, 4, 8, 1, 10, 9, 12, 2, 5, 7

CHAPTER SIX

Listening

1. Two women are standing at a bus stop.

    F, T, F

2. Two friends meet at the beach.

    F, F, F, F, T

3. A national weather announcement on the telephone.

    F, T, F ,F ,F, T

Conversation Practice

2. Scrambled Sentences

    1. 6, 9, 2, 4, 7, 1, 8, 10, 3, 5
    2. 5, 8, 4, 1, 3, 6, 2, 7

Your Turn

2. Weather Expressions

    1. It's bad weather.
    2. It's raining.
    3. It's raining very hard. It's pouring down.
    4. Weather is a common topic of conversation; we have no control over it.
    5. It's raining hard.
    6. If you see a red sky at sunset, the weather will be good the next day. But if you see a red sky in the morning, the weather will be bad that day.

CHAPTER SEVEN

Listening

F, F, T, T ,F, T, F ,F, T, T, T, T, T, T, F, T

Conversation Practice

2. Fill in the blanks.

    1. acoustic   5. soothing
    2. lyrics   6. orchestra
    3. quintet   7. rhythm
    4. modern   8. romantic

3. Matching

    C, A, E, D, B

4. Scrambled Conversation

    6, 4, 8, 2, 9, 7, 1, 3, 5

Chapter Eight

Listening

F, T, F, F, T, F, T, T, F, T, T ,F ,F

Conversation Practice

2. B, A, C

3. B, C, A, F, E, D

4. A, D, B, C

5. C, B, A

6. C, B, A

7. B, A, C

8. C, A, B, D

9. C, A, B

10. Banana, Elephant, Champagne, Saw

CHAPTER NINE

Listening

T, F, F, F, F, T, T, T, F, T, F, T, T

Conversation Practice

2. Matching

    C, O, L, A, E, F, N, K, J, H, D, B, P, G, I

CHAPTER TEN

Listening

F, T, T, F, F, T F, T

Conversation Practice

2. Circle words which can be reduced.

1. (What do you) know (about) South America?
2. (Do you) like sushi?
3. (What are you) (thinking) (about?)
4. I (don't know.)
5. (I want to go) hiking.
6. You (have to) do it!
7. He (ought to be) working.
8. (Do you not) like rock (and) roll?
9. (How are you) (going to) do it?
10. (What did he) say?

Review of CHAPTERS 1-10

1. Conversation Analysis

Conversation One–Worse

No one asks for clarification. Responses are very short. Questions are closed rather than open. There is too much silence. There are no pre-closings. There are no listener expressions.

Conversation Two–Better

Participants ask for clarification and use listener expressions. There are several open questions. The two people answer in detailed sentences. They use pre-closings to finish the conversation. There is no awkward silence.

3. Matching

B, J, E, H, A, G, I, F, C, D

4. Open Questions

2, 3, 5, and 6 are open questions.

5. Vocabulary

1. humid
2. freezing
3. foggy
4. like
5. weather

1. soothing
2. traditional
3. bluegrass
4. acoustic
5. lyrics

1. made from
2. kind of
3. comes from
4. similar to
5. used for

1. bad for you
2. on a diet
3. spicy
4. Why don't we
5. bland

7. Scrambled Conversation

3, 2, 6, 8, 4, 9, 1, 7, 5, 10

CHAPTER ELEVEN

Listening

1. Susie and Bess are discussing the final examinations at their school.

T, F, F, F, T

2. Jeff and Susie are talking after the test.

T, T, F, T, T

3. John and Mike, two college freshmen, meet.

T, T, F, T, T

Conversation Practice

Matching

L, H, N, E, J, M, B, O, D, I, F, G, K, A, C

CHAPTER TWELVE

Listening

1. A couple is sitting in their car in their driveway. They are starting a long trip.

   F ,T, T, F, T, F, F

2. Mel and Ken are talking about a rock concert.

   T, F, T, F, T, T

3. A mother is worried about her child, Sarah.

   T, T, T

Conversation Practice

3. Matching

   G, B, E, F, C, H, A, D

CHAPTER THIRTEEN

Listening

   F, F, T, T, F, T, F, F, T, F, T, T, F

Conversation Practice

2. Fill in the blanks

1. nerd	6. cute
2. redneck	7. jock
3. creep	8. good conversationalist
4. brain	9. mature
5. sweetheart	10. slob

CHAPTER FOURTEEN

Listening

1. Chris and Kevin are walking home from a pizza parlor.

   F, T, F

2. A mother is trying to get her son, Todd to help her.

   F ,T, F, T

3. Eric and Michael are talking.

   T, F, T, T, T, T, F, T, T

Conversation Practice

2. Circle the correct expression.

   Anyway, By the way, So what?, Actually, But, Never mind, and *Anyway*

3. Scrambled Conversation

   8, 4, 2, 10, 3, 12, 9, 13, 1, 6, 11, 5, 7

CHAPTER FIFTEEN

Listening

   F, F, T, T, T, F, T, F, T, F, F, F

Conversation Practice

2. Matching

   J, H, D, A, Q, N, O, R, E, B, L, I, P, M, K, G, F, C

CHAPTER SIXTEEN

Listening

   F, T, F, T, F, T, T ,F, T

Conversation Practice

2. Matching

   E, J, A, G, I, K, M, C, D, F, N, L, H, B

3. Scrambled Conversation

   4, 3, 6, 2, 5, 7, 1

4. Fill in the Blanks

   about, takes place, anyway, Really?, did she do, after, then, got

CHAPTER SEVENTEEN

Listening

   F, T, F, T, F, F, T, T, T, T, F, T, F, T, F, F, T

Conversation Practice

2. Scrambled Sentences

   14, 2, 5, 15, 16, 1, 6, 13, 11, 3, 4, 7, 17, 10, 9, 8, 12

CHAPTER EIGHTEEN

Listening

   F, F, F, T, T, T, F ,F, T, T, F, F, F, F, T, T, F, T

Conversation Practice

2. Fill in the blanks.

1. overtime	9. laid off
2. benefits	10. on the grapevine
3. fired	11. transferred
4. quit	12. headquarters
5. promotion	13. minorities
6. raise	14. apply for
7. bonus	15. paperwork
8. hiring	

CHAPTER NINETEEN

Listening

T, T, F, T, T, T, F, F, T, T, F, F, T, F, T, T

Conversation Practice

2. Fill in the blanks.

1. lousy	11. documentary
2. director	12. scenery
3. game	13. cartoons
4. screenplay	14. comedy
5. action	15. costumes
6. on	16. romances
7. played	17. soap opera
8. about	18. monster
9. cable	19. dramas
10. violent	20. detective

Your Turn

1. Fill in the blanks.

Monster movie, Romance, Detective movie, Foreign film, Comedy, Cartoon

CHAPTER TWENTY

Listening

1. Sergei calls Anna to invite her to a concert.

F, T, T, T, F, F, T, F

2. John calls his classmate, Jackie

F, T, F, F

3. Margarite calls about a job.

F, F, T, T, F, T, F

Conversation Practice

2. Matching

H, J, M, A, N, B, D, E, F, K, G, C, I, L

3. Scrambled Conversations

1. 3, 9, 6, 1, 8, 12, 10, 2, 5, 11, 7, 4
2. 12, 5, 3, 13, 6, 1, 7, 11, 9, 2, 8, 10, 4

Review of CHAPTERS 11-20

1. Scrambled Conversations

4, 13, 6, 17, 3, 15, 8, 16, 10, 11, 1, 2, 7, 12, 5, 14, 9

3. Vocabulary

1. cram
2. flunk
3. Ph.D.
4. goofing off
5. major

1. oops
2. yuck
3. Uh-oh
4. OK
5. ouch

1. slob
2. brain
3. jock
4. redneck
5. sweetheart

1. crazy about
2. sick and tired of
3. homesick
4. get along with
5. upsets

1. affair
2. widow
3. divorce
4. happened
5. married

1. holiday
2. raise
3. hired
4. bonus
5. promotion

1. quit
2. transferred
3. applied
4. incompetent
5. benefits

1. cartoons
2. dramas
3. documentary
4. directed
5. played

1. Tell him
2. Nevermind
3. By the way
4. later
5. actually